Zen
FLOWERS

Zen FLOWERS

DESIGNS TO SOOTHE THE SENSES AND NOURISH THE SOUL

BRENDA BERKLEY & ANULKA KITAMURA   PHOTOGRAPHS BY EMILY BROOKE SANDOR

STEWART, TABORI & CHANG NEW YORK

Editor: Jennifer Levesque
Designer: Julie Hoffer
Production Manager: Jane Searle

Library of Congress Cataloging-in-Publication Data
Berkley, Brenda.
  Zen flowers : designs to soothe the senses and nourish the soul /
Brenda Berkley and Anulka Kitamura ; photographs by Emily Brooke Sandor.
     p. cm.
  Includes index.
  ISBN-13: 978-1-58479-544-5
  ISBN-10: 1-58479-544-1
  1. Flower arrangement, Japanese 2. Zen Buddhism. I. Kitamura,
Anulka. II. Title.

SB450.B47 2006
745.92—dc22   2006010313

Floral designs by Brenda Berkley, Anulka Kitamura, and The Flower Box of Santa Monica, CA
Editorial assistance and project management by Gina Misiroglu

Published in 2006 by Stewart, Tabori & Chang
An imprint of Harry N. Abrams, Inc.

The text of this book was composed in Helvetica Neue and Quiller

Printed and bound in China
10 9 8 7 6 5 4 3 2 1

HNA
harry n. abrams, inc.
a subsidiary of La Martinière Groupe

115 West 18th Street
New York, NY 10011
www.hnabooks.com

Dedicated to my daughter,

KatyRose Berkley Herron,

"Rosebud," a shining bright light in the world.

— Brenda Berkley

To my mother, father, and beautiful family,

the seeds of my being, and for my sons

Koichi and Takashi, the flowering of my heart,

treasures of the universe.

— Anulka Kitamura

Introduction

Life is full of mystery. When I gaze into the throat of an exceptionally beautiful orchid I question how much I know about our amazing world. I do know how flowers make me feel. They have the power to excite, to entrance, to engage. This is the essence of Zen flower arrangement. It represents arranging flowers in a simple, easy manner that allows the life force and innumerable aspects of the flower to be imparted into any space. To design in Zen is to design with the nature of the flower in mind.

The concept of the Zen flower was revealed to me at The Flower Box, my design studio in Santa Monica, California, where I am fortunate enough to bring the beauty of flowers into my clients' homes and offices. While different styles of homes and workspaces require individual design styles, one truth emerged: an approach that imparts the healing and restorative aspects of beautiful flowers is the most exciting design work that I do.

Although I have been in the flower business for more than two decades, I am still amazed at how a single flower can open any heart. I marvel at the wonders of Mother Nature; how dramatically the small touch of her beauty transforms a space from ordinary to spectacular. If we keep it simple, all of us can design beautiful healing flowers. Let the absolute perfect symmetry and proportion of nature be your guide and the magic will unfold.

After working with countless clients across the country, I've developed a timeless approach to floral design; a holistic perspective that has ultimately transformed living spaces, uplifted tired spirits, and nurtured souls. The Zen concept of design is really not a set of rules or exact measurement, but rather a way to look at flowers and consider what they will bring to a space and how best to allow a flower's natural beauty to come through.

In the following pages, you will enjoy learning how to get started with flowers; how to choose from a variety of containers that breathe life into a particular arrangement; how to work with the light, space, and décor of a room; and how a flower's color, texture, shape, and form affect design. You are also invited to embrace the finer points of composition, whether it is the proportion of the flower to the container or several buds in relationship to one another. By blending the concepts of space, balance, proportion, and depth, both beginners and more seasoned naturalists can learn to shape an arrangement. By using simple care and conditioning techniques, you can ensure long-lasting and vibrant floral designs.

Beauty, simplicity, and harmony—these are the cornerstones of Zen flower arranging that are explored in detail in *Zen Flowers.* Through this unique perspective on floral arranging, you can understand how to embrace the ideals and spiritual values of minimalism. The more you clear away and refine the nonessential items and influences in your environment, the better able you are to feel the effects of objects and ideas around you. Allow us to guide you as you explore the varied, sensual worlds of floral design. Discover the many ways in which flowers can nourish the soul, restore the spirit, and bring tranquility and balance to a hectic life.

Zen Flowers is a collaboration with my friend and fellow Buddhist, Anulka Kitamura, who has traveled the world extensively, developing her floral knowledge and a unique take on Zen simplicity. Her love of flowers began in the English countryside where her mother gave each child a small garden plot. Anulka created a lily of the valley and rock garden. One flower . . . one rock. She believed the rock imparted as much life to the garden as did the fragile lily. Anulka traveled to Japan with her husband, Hiroshi Kitamura. There she studied Japanese design and traditions, which she brought to L.A. restaurants Terusushi and Matsuhisa. This book evolved from our separate and shared journeys. We offer it to you for the peace and beauty of your home.

I found flowers in my life at a time when I needed healing. I never overlook that primary connection to the flowers I arrange and purvey; they are pure goodness and love. Flowers will inspire you to create your own sacred spaces, refreshing sanctuaries, and instill a sense of spiritual balance in your life. You will come to cherish their beauty and power.

Brenda Berkley,
The Flower Box, Santa Monica, 2006
Anulka Kitamura, Los Angeles 2006

REFLECTION

If the head and body are to be well,

you must begin by curing the soul.

— Plato

The human spirit has always instinctively embraced the notion that "flowers nourish the soul and soothe the senses." Flowers have the power to affect our minds and our emotions. Flowers reach deep into our hearts with their healing touch. Flowers have been proven to relieve stress, and as such bring a quiet inner peace. When we reflect on a single flower, it can bring up a myriad of emotions.

Flowers have a vast silent language. Floral fragrance evokes sensuality and mood-enhancing energy, while floral essences have cured many ailments. Flowers have the power to ease pain, dissolve anger, and raise a spirit of defeat to one of joy and pure bliss. Orchids, of which there are 20,000 known varieties, have the power to invoke eroticism. "Flower Power" is not only a sixties catch phrase, it is the recognition that flowers have the ability to stir us in ways nothing else in nature can. When we reflect on everything that flowers are, we see that flowers are an integral part of the universe, just as we are.

The great British poet William Blake once wrote, "To see a world in a grain of sand / And a Heaven in a wild flower, / Hold Infinity in the palm of your hand, / And Eternity in an hour . . ." With a Zen flower arrangement, one can expect a myriad of pleasures from a single bloom.

ANCIENT USE AND SIGNIFICANCE
The desire to feel connected to flowers, to name them, and to attach significance

to them has stirred the human soul since time immemorial.

In twelfth-century Japan, letters inscribed on rice paper with *sumi* ink often referred to flowers and nature to encourage and inspire the reader. In India and China, flowers were used to dye silk, cashmere, and rare textiles in indigo blues and saffron golds. Egypt, one of the most ancient civilizations, thrived on the papyrus flower, which symbolizes triumph and joy. Offered to the gods, the fragrant flower yielded many results: baskets, matting, paper, incense, boats, sandals, and bread.

In ancient Greece, athletes were crowned with laurel at the Olympic games. The Greek painter Pausias painted his most famous work, *The Flower Girl*, depicting a young girl holding a wreath of laurel and known as the Garland Weaver. The term "poet laureate" is derived from the tradition of crowning poets with a laurel crown.

An old Egyptian myth professed that the ancient Egyptians used to sing for the lotus in their social gatherings. The ancient Egyptians also used to set aside a day as the feast of the lotus. During this feast, everyone held a silver pot shaped like a lotus with a burning candle in its middle. Optimistic participants walked toward the Nile River with their pots in hand and an overwhelming dream in each of their hearts. According to the myth, if the burning candle floated on the surface of water, the dream would come true.

The lotus flower, also known as the flowering water lily, was the first flower written about in Asian literature. It enjoys the distinction of being the only flower on earth that pollinates itself as it blossoms, signifying the relationship between cause and effect, and suggesting purity and peace. The Lotus Sutra, a sacred scripture of Buddhism (in Sanskrit, *Nam Myoho Renge Kyo*), describes the existence of an innate and universal truth known as the Buddha nature, present in all life. The Sanskrit translation is "devotion to the mystic law of cause and effect through teaching or voice." The Lotus Sutra teaches profound respect for the dignity of all life forms, whether human or otherwise.

THE LANGUAGE OF FLOWERS

Flowers have been messengers around the world for centuries, bearing the most sublime language. In the century before Christ, growing roses was a huge industry, the crop being used to adorn special functions and religious places. Petals were used en masse to surround holy events or to honor special days and events.

Not surprisingly, the flower often took on a very personal meaning. Cleopatra paid a gold coin to fill her room with two feet of perfumed red rose petals, flowers of love, to receive Mark Anthony. Florence Nightingale lifted soldiers' spirits by dispensing flowers to the wounded during World War I. Queen Victoria presented her husband-to-be, Prince Albert, with a flower before their wedding; wanting instinctively to keep the flower close to his heart, he cut a slit in the lapel of his morning coat, creating the first boutonnière.

A language of flowers developed in seventeenth-century Constantinople and in the poetry of Persia. Charles II introduced the Persian poetry to Europe, and in 1716 Lady Mary Wortley Montagu brought the flower language from Turkey to

England. It spread to France and was soon developed into a handbook of 800 floral messages known as the book *Le Language des Fleurs*. Lovers exchanged messages as they gave each other selected flowers or bouquets, and in these bouquets lay an abundance of meaning. A full red rose meant beauty. A white rosebud warned that one is too young for love. Yellow roses signified jealousy, yellow iris stood for passion, filbert suggested reconciliation, and ivy sent a message of marriage.

The Language of Flowers, a game that pondered all the meanings of flowers and their names, was played in many Victorian parlors. Communication with a floral bouquet became a popular way to send secret messages of love and desire in the sexually repressed Victorian era. Each flower and leaf had its own meaning, and lists of floral language thrived and spread.

FROM EAST TO WEST, WE OFFER VARIOUS FLOWERS AND THEIR ESTABLISHED MEANINGS:

ALLIUM	Good fortune and prosperity
ALOE	Healing, affliction
AMARYLLIS	Pride and splendor
ANEMONE	Abandonment
ANGELICA	Inspiration
ANTHURIUM	Intense attraction
APPLE BLOSSOM	Preference
ASTER	Beginnings of greatness
BACHELOR'S BUTTON	Solitude, healing, and hope
BEECH	Grandeur
BIRD OF PARADISE	Strange and wonderful
BROOM	Humility
BUTTERCUP	Childishness and ingratitude
CAMELLIA	Honest excellence
CARNATION	Refusal
CEDAR	Strength
CHRYSANTHEMUM	Hope
COLUMBINE	Folly
COWSLIP	Pensiveness
DAFFODIL	Chivalry
DAHLIA	Instability
DAISY	Innocence
DELPHINIUM	Swiftness and light
DOGWOOD	Endurance
FORGET-ME-NOT	Keepsake
FREESIA	Calm
FOXGLOVE	Youth
GARDENIA	Feminine grace and artistry
GERANIUM	Comfort
GERBERA	Purity
GLADIOLUS	Natural grace
GOOSEBERRY	Anticipation
GRAPE VINE	Drunkenness
HEATHER	Passion
HELIOTROPE	Devotion
HIBISCUS	Seize the opportunity
HOLLY	Foresight
HOLLYHOCK	Fertility
HONEYSUCKLE	Captive love
HYACINTH	Young love
HYDRANGEA	Heartlessness, boasting
IRIS	Message
IVY	Marriage, fidelity
JASMINE	Good luck
LAVENDER	Mistrust
LILAC	Forsaken
LILY	Innocence

LILY OF THE VALLEY	Return of happiness
LOTUS	Silence, chastity
MAGNOLIA	Dignity
MAPLE	Reserve
MARIGOLD	Despair, grief
MIMOSA	Sensitivity
MINT	Virtue
MORNING GLORY	Affection
MUGWORT	Happiness
NARCISSUS	Egotism
OAK	Bravery, hospitality
OLEANDER	Beware
OLIVE	Peace
ORANGE	Generosity
ORCHID	Beauty, ecstasy
PALM	Victory
PANSY	Lovers' thoughts
PEONY	Secrets, prosperity
PERIWINKLE	Promise
PLUMERIA	Aloha
POMEGRANATE	Unspoken desire
POPPY	Dreams
PRIMROSE	Early youth
PROTEA	Challenge of desire
QUEEN ANNE'S LACE	Self-reliance
QUINCE	Temptation
RANUNCULUS	Charm
ROSE (RED)	Love
ROSE (WHITE)	Purity, silence
ROSE (YELLOW)	Friendship
ROSEMARY	Remembrance
SAGE	Domestic virtue
SNAPDRAGON	Presumption
STOCK	Lasting beauty
SUNFLOWER	Power
SWEET PEA	Lasting pleasure
SWEET WILLIAM	Gallantry
SYCAMORE	Curiosity
THYME	Activity
TUBEROSE	Voluptuousness
TULIP	Declare love
VIOLET	Faithfulness
WALNUT	Intellect
WATER LILY	Purity, perfect beauty
WILLOW HERB	Celibacy
WISTERIA	Obedience
WORMWOOD	Absence
ZEPHYR	Expectation
ZINNIA	Sorrow

THE CELEBRATION
AND CEREMONY OF FLOWERS

Flowers, particularly roses, have been used throughout the centuries to help our hearts open and embrace all the lessons that life brings our way. We surround ourselves, almost instinctually, during the worst and best of times, with flowers.

With new beginnings, as we join in matrimony, or when we welcome our newborns into the world, we partake of flowers. When one of us passes on, we send the deceased's loved ones flowers, giving the blessing of their beauty and their elevated vibration. We open people's hearts with our gifts of flowers, whether it

be to declare our love or to seek forgiveness for some emotional transgression. We send flowers as our emissaries on so many emotional missions—in our stead and in our hands.

Flowers have always been an essential part of heralding a celebration. Be it a birth announcement, a wedding, or an anniversary, flowers lend their beauty and fragrance. Great victories are celebrated with the presentation of flowers; wreaths of flowers are placed around the necks of the jubilant. The presence of flowers at any festivity inspires a spirit of celebration and joy.

Events that are sorrowful and evoke deep grief, such as the passing of a loved one, can be made more bearable by the comforting presence of flowers. Posies are handled with reverence and deliver much more than words ever can. Bouquets of roses are presented as symbols of mourning; the transience of flowers links the deceased with immortality. We remember loved ones by the flowers they cherished, and as such they become memorial flowers. They are placed with great love and care on the casket or grave of the deceased who has passed on from this life to the next destination in the infinite realm of eternity. After cremation, ashes are often distributed, followed by a sprinkling of flower petals.

THE POWER OF A SINGLE ROSE

Greek and Roman legends state that the rose is the very creation of the gods. Indeed, it is the flower most associated with divinity and is the embodiment of the essence of a "higher" consciousness. Roses are well known throughout time to be almost magical in their medicinal, spiritual, and healing powers. More than 4,000 years ago, rose oil and water were mandatory items in most tombs of Egyptian royalty, who felt both were absolutely necessary in the afterlife. The teachings of Buddha championed horticulture and encouraged one to cultivate a garden full of roses to aid in one's spiritual growth.

Aside from their obvious striking beauty and fragrance, which heal the spirit, open the heart, and soothe the mind, the rose holds one of the highest energy vibrations ever recorded. Rose oil is used to bless our newborns to help them transition into this world. We anoint our dead to surround them with a protective shield of the energy of love, which is the energy of the rose, and its high vibration again aids in the transition home, back to Nirvana or Heaven. Roses, like all flowers and plants, are like any living form: they reflect back into the world what is put into them and impart these aspects wherever they are. Roses are a small glimpse of the Divine.

SEASONAL REPRESENTATIONS

Since pagan times, the month of May has been celebrated with the adorning of the maypole, which is decorated with garlands of flowers. Dancers, with flowers in their hair, dance around the tall pole and welcome spring and its abundance. The ceremony also celebrates life, the maypole representing the male organ and the dancers the seeds of life. In France, on May Day it is a traditional custom to give a small posy of lily of the valley to friends as a token to celebrate the end of winter and to welcome spring.

Each season welcomes its own flowers as it marks new beginnings. And each season has its own festive celebration, be it the spring equinox, summer solstice, autumn equinox, or winter solstice. The Zen flower has its place in each. Nichiren said, "Winter never fails to turn into spring." Worldwide, spring heralds joy and life.

Flowering bulbs—hyacinth, crocus, daffodils, narcissus—and a host of roses, camellias, and primroses push their shoots through the earth and open their beautiful floral heads in the spring sun, their colors and fragrances abounding.

Meadows are lush with cowslip, heather, violets, bluebells, and sage. Trees are bursting with blossoms in anticipation of the fruit to come. They scent the spring air and welcome baby birds.

We feel renewed and alive; spring feels like a time to celebrate life and abundance. Around the world, spring is heralded with floral arrangements—both simple and complex—comprising peonies, peach, apple, and cherry blossoms, tulips, jasmine, gardenias, bougainvillea, hollyhocks, hydrangeas, and a host of golden daffodils.

The event of the spring equinox, when the sun is directly above the earth's equator, has been celebrated the world over for thousands of years. All cultures hold spring festivals. In Persia, equinox is one of the oldest traditions, celebrated as the New Year. During equinox, there is an awakening of the earth; animals emerge from hibernation and the resurrection of budding and blooming occurs.

Spring is the season of impromptu picnics, spring teas, lunches, and light suppers, with Zen floral arrangements

gracing the events. Experiment with all the flowers that spring has to offer as you assemble your Zen arrangements.

Summer brings wildly fragrant lilacs, roses in thousands of colors and scents, rosemary, lavender, irises, citrus blossoms, sweet pea, tulips, delphiniums, cream magnolias, and orchids of all colors and styles. The fields are full of marigolds, burdock, chamomile, buttercups, dandelion, and arnica, all beautiful flowers with great healing powers. Flowers collected, squeezed for precious oils, and made into fragrances are worn by men and women the world over.

Summer solstice is the longest day of the year. *Sol* means "sun" and *sistere* means "to stand still," as the sun appears to stand still the longest on this day. The warm temperatures bring an abundance of blooming flowers. Bees work tirelessly to bring honey to the hive. June 21 is the traditional day to collect honey from the hive, when it is filled to capacity. On this day, the moon is also called the "honey moon," which is why many marriages traditionally have occurred on summer solstice, followed with a honeymoon.

Throughout the world, summer is a time of abundance. From North Africa to Scandinavia, the summer is celebrated with fire festivals generating sympathetic magic and giving a boost to the sun's energy, so that it will remain strong and potent, and to guarantee a plentiful harvest.

In ancient China, summer embraced the earth's *yin* force. Feminine young ladies—too delicate to mix with the general public—stood on balconies and tossed bouquets of flowers with streaming ribbons to the men of their choosing, signaling their desire for love.

The Native American Natchez tribe worshipped the sun and believed that life descended from it. Each summer they held a fruit and flower ceremony, and only harvested their corn after the feast.

In Poland, young girls made wreaths of sweet pea and herbs with candles in the middle and sent them adrift down the river to bring husbands. Variations on these ancient customs still abound today. A Zen floral design of tall lotus flowers, a single bloom of orchids, or a mass of blue agapanthus all signify summer. In summer, the azurine collection of flowers is at its best, with lavender, cornflowers, forget-me-nots, sweet pea, penstemons, eryngium, perovskia, and echinops all gracing a summer solstice feast.

Albert Camus mused, "Autumn is a second spring when every leaf is a flower." As the spring and summer blossoms depart and the autumn wind takes hold, maple leaves turn fiery red and flowers abound. Dahlia, chrysanthemums, gladiolus, sweet-smelling narcissus, rich velvet lilies, and deep burnt gold and orange gourds and squash bring a warm-toned richness to our environment.

Autumn is the time of year when the earth is balanced. Days and nights are the same length of time and harmony produces harvest. Autumn harvest is cou-

pled with final gathering. It is a time when reflection manifests itself.

Reflection is a fundamental tenet of Buddhism. The Serene Reflection Meditation tradition (in Japan, *Soto Zen*) is the oldest tradition found within Zen Buddhism. It was brought from China and introduced into Japan by the thirteenth-century Great Master Dogen. This teaching stresses the practice of meditation, the necessity of keeping the Buddhist precepts, and the unity of training and enlightenment. Although the external form of Buddhist

practice has changed and adapted to each particular culture as Buddhism moved from India to China, to Japan, and now to the West, the essence of the Buddha's teachings remains unchanged.

Every culture welcomes autumn in its own way. People the world over make symbols of gathered straw and grain. Harvest queens are hung in homes to embody the spirit of the crop and ensure abundance. It is the time of Thanksgiving, Sukkot, Ramadan, and the Diwali festivals, when Hindus adorn themselves

and decorate their homes with hundreds of flowers. In Japan it is the time for Momijari, or "leaf watching," as the green transforms to gold, burgundy, orange, yellow, and fiery reds.

The autumn equinox is the season for families and cultures to come together. It signifies a time of reflection, an appreciation for the harvest, and a preparatory time for the coming winter months. Flowers and long-lasting produce are bountiful and should be used with bold confidence in any Zen floral arrangement.

Branches of oak, maple, and golden miniature pumpkins are great accents to any home. Homes and tables overflow with pumpkins, pomegranates, gourd squashes, chestnuts, and berries. Simple arrangements of cockscombs, huge dark dahlias, golden chrysanthemums, cream lilies, hibiscus, and the fragrant jasmine and honeysuckle flowers all reflect autumn's warmth, bringing a feeling of rich festivity to any environment.

In a time that otherwise feels cold and barren, winter delivers tall and strong amaryllis, prickly holly with bright red berries, camellias, witch hazel, burnt brown and burgundy calla lilies, heavily perfumed jasmine and gardenias, delicate paper-white narcissus, mistletoe, pine and fir, and endless poinsettias.

Winter solstice marks long nights and short days. From Roman times, people have welcomed winter with a determination to keep a light or fire burning until the spring arrives. Lamps were burned to ward off spirits of darkness. Yule fires and candles were kept lit all winter long.

The Emperor Aurelian established December 25 as the Invincible Sun Day; since then, pagan and Christian customs have merged to celebrate the coldest month of winter with many ancient traditions and customs. The Chinese, in *Ja Dung*—winter—paint a plum tree with 81 colorless flowers; each day, one is painted red until the painting is complete.

Queen Victoria appeared in an illustration with her family in front of a Christmas tree in the *London News*, creating a tradition worldwide of erecting a Christmas tree in the home, decorated with paper flowers: red for knowledge and white for innocence. Ribbons and glass ornaments were added, as were lights representing the twinkling stars of the night.

Chanukah is a festival of lights, whereby a new candle is lit in a Menorah for each of eight consecutive days. Kwanzaa is also a festival celebratd with lights. Kwanzaa means "first fruits of the harvest." Seven candles are placed in a candelabrum called a *kinara* to represent the seven principles of this African-American festival.

Native Americans celebrate winter solstice by crafting prayer sticks. Each one, made out of a cedar branch from a tree that one feels connected to, is planted in the ground with the name of an ancestor, a turkey feather, and tobacco.

In the Zen tradition, evergreens are of great importance, as they symbolize eternity and the continuity of the life cycle. Participants make wreaths of laurel, holly, fir, and birch and place candles in their centers. People often fashion Yuletide wreaths. Mistletoe is considered a plant of good luck because it grows on the "lucky oak."

In the past, it was hung above doorways of homes to bring good fortune; a kiss under the mistletoe is a pledge of friendship.

Juniper, holly, pine, birch, cedar, spruce, ivy, and fir are significant plants for Zen arrangements in winter. Winter flowers include amaryllis, crocus, snowdrops, narcissus, iris, witch hazel, ilex berries, cloves, cinnamon, and nutmeg, all of which add fragrant spice flavors and brightness to cold winter nights. One can make simple yet provocative arrangements with any or all of these wintertime treasures, particularly if one is careful not to overstock the container.

THE HEALING EFFECTS OF FLOWERS

The healing power of plants and flowers is profound. Having graced the planet for 100 million years, they soothe, stimulate, and inspire the human soul. Their energy is seemingly transmitted to us when we touch them; their fragrances affect our brains, hearts, and souls at the deepest emotional level. And as we feast our eyes on their pure perfection, their beautiful colors and shapes fill us up in yet another way: Flowers open our hearts to feel love.

All of us have personally benefited from

FLOWERS TO NOURISH THE SOUL

An old Chinese proverb says, "When you have only two pennies left in the world, buy a loaf of bread with one and a lily with the other." There is something to be said for the necessity of flowers in our lives as life-giving agents that both nourish the soul and feed the inner being.

Flowers possess the ability to alter our consciousness, change our mood, uplift our emotions. Arranging flowers can be a very healing, restorative, calming, and grounding process. The essence of the flowers, the feel of them, the visual beauty, the wonder of their creation—all of these things come together to create an opportunity to clear one's mind, to breathe, to let go of the outcome, and revel in the process of creativity and design. Flowers stir us deep in our souls.

the healing effect of flowers, whether we are aware of this fact or not. All flowers have healing properties of one type or another. A flower such as hypericum, which florists use as a beautiful berrylike accent, is actually St. John's wort, a remedy commonly used for depression. This medicinal aspect of the plant is imparted as a cut flower and can help lift one's spirits. Peonies are "the women's healing flower" in Chinese herbal medicine because many parts of it are used to cure feminine ailments. And we have never met a woman who didn't love cut peonies delivered to her doorstep! Solidago is a commonly used bright yellow cheerful filler; few know that its medicinal name is echinacea, commonly used to thwart the first signs of a cold or flu.

Simply put, flowers are cheerful. They affect us through their colors, fragrances, shapes, and vibrational quality. They are the cure when nothing else will do.

FLOWERS TO RESTORE THE SPIRIT

Spirituality and flowers are inseparable. The Buddha was born floating on a lotus leaf. In the Hindu religion, Brahma also was born in the bosom of the lotus, which represents the cradle of the universe. The rose of Jericho, or the rose of Mary, first blossomed when Christ was born. Cedar, cypress, and palm made up the cross. Mohammed called henna the chief of flowers. From his perspiration, freshly fallen from paradise, sprang both rice and the rose.

Yet flowers do more than symbolize the divine. With flowers, we can raise our vibrations and open our spiritual self. When flowers surround us, we are reminded of the presence of something larger than ourselves, a bigger perspective. We are reminded to look up, to look outward beyond the finite. When we look at a flower we are almost always brought to an awe-inspired pause in our hectic lives; when one truly pauses to look at a blossom one is reminded of all that is

good. We all hold in us the very essence of life, godliness, the Buddha, the creator in us. The beauty of a flower in our presence brings this forth in our lives. It elevates our expectations. It enhances our loving actions. It can simply make us smile.

That is why cultures both past and present have always propagated and employed flowers in so many ways. We adorn ourselves, our marriages, our births, and our deaths with flowers. We celebrate with flowers, we announce with flowers, we ask our most important questions with gorgeous blossoms. We thank with them. We heal in many ways with flowers, we adorn our religious cathedrals, temples, and churches with them. They inspire us to give, to express, to honor—they are the only touch that will do for so many of our most precious human moments. They are a breath of the heavens and stars. As the blessings of the gods, we bring them, we send them, we pile them up high. All this from the grace, beauty, and magic of a flower.

PREPARATION

Whatever you think you can do or believe you can do, begin it.

For in action there is magic, grace and power.

—Goethe

Every beautiful Zen arrangement begins somewhere. As one contemplates the perfect arrangement, a string of thoughts or an idea surfaces. In order to transform these thoughts into reality, preparation must become the cornerstone to one's design.

In every Zen design, organization is key: calmness of mind, and an organization of your environment, your tools, and the flowers themselves. Here, as never before, the old adage rings true: "Out of order exudes creativity."

The Zen approach to preparedness includes an acute awareness of one's inborn senses. Be ready to engage your senses of sight, smell, and touch as you begin your floral arrangements. Invite into your consciousness an intentional desire to bring nature and its beauty into your surroundings. The decision to invoke life into an environment should be a voyage of exploration and pleasure without stress or fuss. Relax, enjoy, and begin!

GETTING STARTED: CLEARING YOUR MIND

Clearing one's mind and uncluttering the workspace provide the opportunity to delve into the world of serenity and harmony. A Zen approach to flowers is one of simplicity and an appreciation of the beauty of a single stem, a leaf, a curly willow, chosen to accent a tiny environment or a large, open space. No matter what the end goal of a floral design, the preparation of one's thinking is as important as the preparation of one's workspace.

Clearing the mind does not require being anywhere other than where one is in body and spirit at a particular moment. So, a formal, meditative state is not a necessary one. In readying yourself to begin your arrangement, start with the simple thought of what a joy it is to encounter a beautiful flower and use it to bring life to your living space. Look closely at the bud. Revel in the peculiarity of the stem or leaf. Breathe in the fragrance of the flower. Because the human life force and nature's life force are inextricably connected, it is essential to embrace the living, breathing entity of the flower. The realization that we are both alive and connected, infused by the same oxygen, relying on the same sources for light and water, is what makes the preparatory process uplifting.

To fully absorb the benefits of the live materials you are working with, focus on the task at hand. Breathe deeply. Free yourself of worry, fear, and the daily constraints of living. Relax and allow the flowers and greens to go where they want to, where it seems natural and easy. This is not a time to be critical of yourself, but rather a time to have fun! Realize that not only are you creating beauty in your home or business, you are shifting the energy there. Your results will affect in a positive way everyone who enters, even if they are not fully conscious of what moves them.

Linked with freeing one's mind is the concept of peace and tranquility. Take your time. Do not rush the creative process; yet, at the same time, know that you can indeed create a beautiful arrangement in the fifteen minutes you have between preparing your hors d'oeuvres and setting the dinner table. Time, as measured by minutes on the clock, is not the point; rather, we are talking about approaching your arrangement with an unhurried state of mind.

PREPARING YOUR WORKSPACE

Any clean, flat area close to running water will suffice. Before you begin, take a few deep breaths and clear off your space. Whether you are working on a kitchen counter, a large picnic table in your backyard, or a plank of wood stacked on two barrels in your garage, the message remains the same: Be organized. A clean, well-lit space with only the necessary items will exude the feeling of order and tranquility—both key to the Zen approach.

The height of your workspace is important to both your physical comfort and the success of the design. Your shoulders should be relaxed and your line of sight at approximately the same level that the arrangement will be viewed from. When designing centerpieces, further elevate your container from the usual height with a small stool so that as you design the piece you will be viewing it from the same angle that it will be seen by guests when it is placed on the table.

Wipe down your space with a clean cloth and light disinfectant, such as a few drops of essential oil of lavender diluted in a half-gallon of water. Organize your tools. You'll find that having the right items, clean and at your fingertips, goes a long way toward helping you structure your thoughts. An organized, well-lit surface provides you with the practical space you'll need to trim your stems, work with your materials and equipment, and arrange your design.

At The Flower Box, we often use large earthen containers (available at most local gardening shops or home-repair warehouses) to hold clippers, wire, foam, and other necessities. The earthen vessel, made of clay or stone, organically connects one to the earth. Stock up on your essentials and have them in your visual consciousness.

Likewise, even in the smallest of workspaces, reserve a cabinet or a shelf for your favorite vases, containers, and vessels—those special items made of crystal, china, or clay that you feel work best in your space. Having your vessels within arm's reach during the design process is key; when you are through with them, wash and dry them thoroughly.

A note about the wall or area behind your workspace: Try to strive for a neutral tone behind your design space or table. A neutral color will not compete with your floral design, and will better allow you to see the lines and spaces you are creating.

Once you have your workspace prepared, it's time to buy your tools and materials.

CHOOSING TOOLS AND MATERIALS

Tools should be efficient, made for the task at hand, and as ergonomically correct as possible. A great pair of shears is essential for any designer, and the one investment truly worth making. Other materials that may prove invaluable include pin holders (frogs), florist foam (oasis), wire mesh (netting), floral wire and spikes, florist arranging tape, floral putty, and water tubes. Aesthetic accessories that also serve a practical function in supporting the flower stem include stones, pebbles, curly willow, twigs, driftwood, sand, shells, and raffia.

CUTTING TOOLS: As convenient as they are to pick up, household scissors are not the correct tool for cutting flowers. Our favorite tool for floral design is a pair of *ikebana* shears by Kengyu, available from most mail-order outlets and well-stocked gardening retailers. They are easy to use, make a nice clean cut to insure good water uptake for the flower, and remain sharp for a long time. They will cut almost any type of flower or plant. For the larger, more woody stems such as proteas, try an anvil pruner made by a reputable company such as Corona.

Another wonderful tool for design is the floral knife, but it requires a higher level of skill to use. The knife should be sharp and not too large. The knife is per-fect for removing thorns from roses, shoots from bamboo, knots on a pear- or apple-blossom branch, and excess foliage from just about any leafy flower. When stripping the debris away from the flower stem, use a downward-motion stroke, cutting away from your upper body. The result is a crisp, clean finish.

Keep domestic scissors on hand for cutting tape, string, or paper. A regular household hammer is often used for crushing the ends of wooden stems, as with blossoms, dogwood, and lilac.

A good washing with soap and water will keep tools virus and fungus free. Be sure to give them a thorough drying. Olive oil is a wonderful lubricant should you need to condition them.

PIN HOLDERS (FROGS): The pin holder is a weighty, metal disc that comes in many different diameters, with sharp metal pins inside. Colloquially called a "frog" in the floral business, this item is very useful in the bottom of a container when one wishes to have flowers stand independently upright. Each flower is pushed onto a pin, making the frog ideal for linear designs. Frogs are also key in creating a sense of space within the container, helping to define the lines of both vessel and flower.

The weight of the frog will support the weight of most flowers and keep the arrangement balanced. In the event that you are working with a very heavy bloom, such as proteas, secure the frog in the bottom of the container with floral putty.

FLORIST FOAM (OASIS): Florist foam, or oasis, comes in a vast variety of shapes and colors. It is very lightweight, porous, and easy to handle. It can be cut to a desired shape with a floral knife. Key to working with floral foam is the preparation. Soak the foam in water for up to an hour until there are no visible air bubbles in the water. Remove the foam and place it in the base of your container. Floral foam works best in non glass vessels, unless you camouflage it with leaves or the like.

WIRE MESH: Available for pennies, wire mesh is an indispensable material that can be used alone to create somewhat architectural designs. It should be cut from the roll, slightly crumpled, and placed inside the vessel. Wire mesh does not work well with large, stemmed flowers.

FLORAL WIRE AND WOODEN SPIKES: Floral wire and spikes can be used to strengthen or shape a stem, as typically seen with flowers that tend to droop, such as Gerbera daisies. Spikes are useful for pushing into fruit or vegetables, when these items are used to accent an arrangement, or for pushing into the heads of flowers in a shallow-dish design. Because wiring may shorten the life of the flower (as it pierces the veins that transport water to the bloom), use it selectively.

FLORAL TAPE: Floral tape can be used for just about any design. Available almost everywhere for pennies, it is useful for camouflaging the joints of flowers and wires or sticks. When wrapped around a stem in a spiraling motion, the tape will stick due to the heat from your hands. Tape will also enable a wired flower to retain moisture. It comes in many different colors, green being the most versatile.

WATER TUBES: These plastic vials, sold in packs of varying sizes, are an inexpensive way to be creative with one's designs. Utilizing an individual blossom (perhaps one that has fallen from the stem and might otherwise be discarded), simply tuck the bloom inside a water-filled tube. One can either accent an existing arrangement or use a flower in a tube to garnish a dinner napkin or a loved one's pillow. Tubes have endless possibilities and are perfect for miniature roses, orchids, and lilies: Stick them in an unconventional vessel that doesn't hold water or distribute them in select places in your home or business.

ACCESSORIES: Stones, pebbles, curly willow, twigs, driftwood, sand, shells, and raffia serve the dual function of being both beautiful and practical. Borrowing from the Zen concept of minimalism and dual function, these accessories—lifted from all facets of nature—enliven arrangements and provide a base of support to the floral stem.

SELECTING A FLOWER SOURCE

The flowers available today are more varied than ever, with both specialty florists and garden shops importing unique blooms from around the globe. Access to flowers is no longer seasonal, but available year-round, as a quick survey of your local grocery's floral section will attest. Flowers are grown commercially and in great quantity. Once rare and expensive, flowers like the orchid have become readily available throughout the world and at reasonable cost. Exotics and calla lilies are available year-round in abundance. The following represent a variety of both big-city and suburban sources available to almost everyone:

YOUR LOCAL FLORIST: Choose a local florist with a good reputation, perhaps based upon a recommendation from a friend or colleague who has purchased arrangements there. Your local florist can help you locate that exotic white tulip anthurium, hanging haliconia from the Hawaiian island of Maui, or the perfect pastel-pink peony. A neighborhood florist can be a wealth of advice and information on a variety of topics, from selection to care and conditioning. A knowledgeable florist has their finger on the sources of the best, freshest, and longest-lasting blooms, and likely they will have a grooming tip up their sleeve for the asking. Unlike those at a your local grocery or convenience market, a good florist's stems are rarely "picked over," ensuring a great selection. Truly, the best way to create a beautiful design is to start with gorgeous, fresh product that requires little to make it shine.

The concept of relationship is key to working with a local florist. Get to know the owner and his or her staff. Discuss your living space with them, and discuss the goals of your arrangements, even if it is a simple, "I'd like a single stem for my bedside table." If the proprietor of the shop gets to know your needs, then he or she can serve you all the better.

YOUR LOCAL GROCERY: One should not resist the temptation to pick up a bouquet of daisies along with the newspaper, especially if one is in the mood or a special friend is stopping by for a visit. Simply be aware of the limitations of flowers from your local grocery store. Likely, they aren't as fresh as they could be, having traveled several days by truck to reach their destination. However, organic whole-foods markets or specialty shops (such as those that serve up cappuccinos and spring blooms) often have

a surprisingly fresh array of bouquets. The key to buying ready-made bouquets involves imagining the bouquet "undone" and rearranged with your signature style. Often, we suggest buying two bouquets of the same type, disassembling them, and picking and choosing what to reassemble. This will give you more of one type of flower for a simpler, more elegant look. Or, if they are available, try purchasing several bouquets of one kind of flower. and create your own design.

THE OUTDOOR FARMERS' MARKET: The local farmers' market is another good source for buying flowers. Strolling through an open-air market filled with the colors and scents of organic vegetables, fruits, and flowers can be a heady, even exotic, experience—and the appeal to the senses will inspire you with boundless design ideas. Unlike your local florist, however, flowers in an open-air market are displayed outside, exposed to the elements, and moved frequently from location to location. Although they may cost less than other sources, they generally are not as strong as florist flowers that are kept at a regulated temperature and nestled in one fixed location. Flowers love tranquility, and the less they are shuffled around, the longer they live.

Here is where *context* plays a role in one's choice of purchasing locale: If looking for statuesque sunflowers to adorn the corner of a living room, then purchasing them at your local farmers' market

certainly won't hurt; if the arrangement is for a special affair, such as a celebration dinner or welcome-home party, or if you simply want a more elegant arrangement, choose the freshest flowers from the most reputable source possible.

WHOLESALE FLOWER MARKET: The wholesale flower market is truly a delight for the soul. Typically, one must obtain a resale license to purchase flowers at the wholesale market, but many frequently offer later hours for customers who do not have one. The availability of product is almost overwhelming—and it is so much fun to venture into an environment that one typically doesn't frequent. In addition, wholesale venues offer great tools and floral supplies; so, while selecting one's favorite lilies, one can also stock up on boxes of floral foam at reasonable cost.

YOUR OWN BACKYARD: Anyone who has grown a patio garden or full-fledged English extravaganza can attest to the joy of harvesting nature's beauty. Plants that one has lovingly tended, watered, and nurtured bring deep satisfaction when snipped for inclusion in a tabletop arrangement. The backyard or container garden often provides that unusual twist of nature that rarely gets selected for big retailers—the bent stem, the uniquely colored petal, the apprehensive bud. These oddities of nature breathe life into an arrangement and free it from convention,

and as such should not be overlooked. In addition, gardens provide the opportunity to snip a piece of ornamental grass, a slice of jade, or a vibrant spring flower—several nontraditional accents for an arrangement that only you can hand select.

BUYING FLOWERS ONLINE: The World Wide Web can be a rewarding source for purchasing flowers if one can locate and access growers selling their flowers directly to online consumers. However, second- or third-party online sellers often disappoint the discerning customer—or the one who simply wants to hand select the flowers he or she is buying. The critical component of using one's senses of sight, touch, and smell is missing from online shopping, causing many designers to use this source as a low-priority option. Still, if you don't have time to run to your local source for a snippet of bear grass, ordering selectively online can be a great time saver. Just be cognizant of additional costs, such as shipping and handling.

Finding the right source for the freshest flowers is important, but it is not the only factor that affects the life of the arrangement. Not only do the flowers and greens impart energy to the environment, but they respond to the way they are treated as well. Flowers truly respond to the touch. Always approach your design and the wonders that Mother Nature has provided with a strong sense of appreciation and love for them, and they will in kind reward you with an extended life and enhanced vibrancy.

HANDPICKING YOUR FLOWERS

No matter what the source, the flowers you choose should be fresh (look for buds just beginning to open), with green unblemished leaves and no missing petals. Flower petals should never appear wrinkled, and fading color is a clear indicator of an older flower. Yellowing of petals or blossoms also indicates age.

TULIPS: Look for fresh, closed buds. An older tulip will have an open bud and a slender, almost transparent stem just below the blossom.

ROSES: In general, roses should have healthy, green leaves, and there should be no decay or mold at the base of the petals (a condition called viritus). A lack of foliage, or yellow foliage, is a sign of an older rose.

LILIES: Look for a sturdy, thick stem with strong, closed (or semiclosed) buds and dark green leaves. With a fresh lily, one should not detect limpness, shriveling, or withering.

BASIC HANDLING TECHNIQUES

Gentle handling and respect for the life of a flower is key. Correctly readying your flowers for their arrangement will enhance their longevity and contribute to their vibrancy. No matter the end design or what flowers one has selected, some basic handling techniques apply: Once you purchase your flowers, it is important to keep them out of the sun and elements until you are ready to design.

• Keep a bucket of fresh water at your side at all times. Keeping the flowers in fresh water will breathe life into them after a tiring journey home.

• Unbundle and then cut them, preferably under water, to prevent air from traveling up the stem. Then place them in fresh water immediately, and allow them to drink. After the flowers have had a chance to rehydrate, recut the stems at an angle, again preferably under water. Exceptions to this rule are flowers that have traveled long distances—and have often been shipped out of water at least overnight—such as Ecuadorian roses or Dutch tulips. Their stems need to firm up in their packaging in order retain their correct shape once unbundled.

• Flowers should be cleaned of soil and debris and any natural clutter prior to placing them inside the bucket. Some flowers, such as hydrangea (which drink through both their petals and stems) and antherium (which drink through their stamens) can actually be completely submerged in water for a time for a full rehydration. Also, it is important to remove the lower leaves from the stem so they are not standing in water, inviting the growth of bacteria, which will cause the leaves to rot.

• Many flowers enjoy a light spritz of water to help rehydrate the petals.

• When using your floral shears to cut the flower, stay focused. Be conscious of the kind of stem you are working with; some are soft and flexible and others strong and will require more pressure with the cut. Either way, cutting the stem at an angle allows the water and its nutrients to enter the flower more readily than a strictly horizontal cut.

• If you wish to create a quick pick-me-up for a tired flower, add one to two drops of household bleach per gallon of water. This simple formula retards decay of the stem and allows the flower to continue to drink for a longer time. It also helps with the clarity of the water. Bleach is more effective than sugar or aspirin, which cloud the water and can increase decay. You may also choose to purchase a commercial floral additive to enhance the length of the life of the arrangement.

SPECIALTY TECHNIQUES

The following specialty techniques work miracles with arrangements, and are simple and fun:

WARM WATER: Recutting and placing a flower in warm water—or in a warm location—encourages a reluctant bud to open. This technique works well to accelerate the opening of certain flowers, such as lilies, irises, and peonies, or to help bring more color to bulb flowers, such as hyacinth, tulips, and freesia.

REFLEXING: If your roses are too tight, you can try "reflexing" the petals. This technique involves opening the petals by placing your thumb into the center of the outside of the petal and gently rolling the petal over your thumb. This forces the rose to open outward, displaying its color and beauty more prominently, and making it appear much larger. This is especially advantageous for party work.

GENTLY FORCING FLOWERS OPEN: Once a bud is showing color, you can "force" it to open by carefully separating

THE CREATIVE ENVIRONMENT

The Zen floral-design approach relies on the principles of embracing the environment and using the properties of the flower—color, balance, scale, proportion, shape, and texture—to bring out the best in both the flower and the arrangement. These topics are covered in detail in the chapters that follow. Here are a few tips on tapping into your inner creativity and utilizing the best your environment has to offer:

the petals along the seam. Irises respond well to this technique: Peel back the green exterior shell of the iris; then tap the bottom of the stem on a firm surface and it will pop the flower open. When using this technique with lilies, you can remove the stamen at the same time, in order to keep the pollen from staining the flower or anything it might come into contact with.

MUSIC: Listening to music while designing is a very individualistic choice. Depending on one's mood, one can get into the spiritual zone of creating with a simple Japanese flute, classical Strauss, or environmental sounds of nature. Rock, blues, world, punk, and funk evoke different emotions and sensations in different people, and can make the design process a vibrant or soothing one. At

The Flower Box, we run the gamut from Norah Jones to Pavarotti, to Led Zeppelin, and to Bob Marley.

MOOD ENHANCERS: Besides playing music, one might want to burn a few candles, steep a hot cup of herbal tea, sip a glass of fine wine, or light some incense before beginning. However, be sensitive to the fragrance of the flowers and avoid invoking any mood enhancers that compete with the flowers' natural aroma. Especially fragrant blooms and greens—such as tuberoses, lilac, lavender, lilies, rosemary, and eucalyptus—stamp their own signature upon a room, exuding a distinct scent that the thoughtful designer is careful not to intrude upon.

LIGHTING: If your workspace is not well lit by either natural or artificial lighting, we suggest adding a light source. Soft, incandescent bulbs are best; the idea is to invite enough light without creating a glare or casting shadows on your work. One must be sensitive to the flowers' needs as well. For example, consider how much light and heat your arrangement will be subject to. Flowers vary greatly in their ability to endure heat and light. Tropical, exotic, and summer flowers—such as orchids, birds of paradise, haliconia, ginger, protea, tuberoses, blossom woods, sunflowers, or flowers that are continuing to open—typically endure heat better than flowers grown in cooler climates or shade, like hydrangea, roses, lisianthus, or flowers with delicate, dry blossoms.

VESSELS

In Zen there are no elaborations,

it aims directly at the true nature of things.

There are no ceremonies; no teachings;

the prize of Zen is essentially personal.

—Victor Harris

Every beautiful Zen arrangement is somehow contained. Containers, or vessels as they are eloquently termed, come in a wide variety of shapes and sizes. One glance around one's home or office will more than likely yield a myriad of options—be they pots, glass vases, tall ceramic cylinders, an old garden urn, a favorite Fiestaware pitcher, a Baccarat crystal wineglass—even a porcelain teacup. Almost anything that will hold water is a candidate.

Vessels need not be elaborate or expensive. Every container yields its own element of individuality and beauty. And every container is guaranteed to come alive with the addition of a fresh blossom.

Key concepts when choosing a vessel are enthusiasm, experimentation, and spontaneity. Don't hesitate to try something new. While it is quite possible that a standard glass cylinder is the perfect choice for an arrangement, a shallow ceramic dish might be equally impressive. The vessel's proportion, size, shape, and style are all considerations that will ultimately contribute to the uniqueness of a Zen flower design, and a correct choice will be as apparent as a misstep. Vessels are interchangeable; if your original selection isn't quite right, you can always substitute another.

ELEMENTS OF THE EARTH, ELEMENTS OF THE VESSEL

In the centuries-old Zen design tradition, scholars acknowledged the five elements of water, wood, fire, metal, and earth as the key components of the physical world.

Each living entity—be it human, animal, or plant—has a relationship with the five elements. A flower, which came from the earth and water, and which returns to the water in its vessel, is connected to its native physical and spiritual world. The following elements represent these qualities:

WATER: The energies that flow through the cycle of life, bringing new beginnings, courage, and confidence. Water, with its ever-changing ebbing and flowing, its yin and yang, represents the essence of life

WOOD: Tranquility, spirituality, inner development; brings strength during stress and sicknesses.

FIRE: Courage, passion, expressionism. Connects us with a higher purpose; necessary to create pottery, glass, ceramics, and china.

METAL: Open-heartedness, clarity, wisdom, strength.

EARTH: Support from the universe; balance, nurturing, stability, from which life is given.

Recognizing the vessel's attributes inevitably brings an appreciation for the materials with which one is working.

SIX CORE CHOICES: CERAMICS, GLASS, STONE, TERRA-COTTA, WOOD, WICKER

The beauty of the vessel as an art form—and its success as a part of the total arrangement—depends in part on the element from which it is made. A square stone pot, an oblong ceramic dish, a tall wooden cylinder, or an antique silver vase embraces an intrinsic quality and evokes certain emotions. With the addition of a stem or stems of flowers, branches, and grasses, one can create a simple and striking arrangement that brings harmony to its environment.

CERAMICS, FROM INDIGENOUS POTTERY TO FINE BONE CHINA:

Ceramics come in a wide variety of styles of designs, depending upon their craftsman and country of origin. The 30,000-year-old art of ceramics includes everything from South American pottery to American art pottery of the Craftsman period, to fine European bone china. Ceramic containers are created by artists and companies with distinct artistic goals, designs, colors, and glazes, and each one has its own flavor and contribution. Ceramics were born out of the discovery of the combination of fire and clay. As such, ceramics capture the essence of Zen, whether classical or modern. Each piece embodies the life force of the artist, through his or her hands to ours.

The scope of ceramics is so varied that it is virtually impossible to lay down a list of dos and don'ts when working with them. Choose a vessel with a strong

finish that holds water without leaking . . . or be willing to improvise. Because the finishes and glazes of ceramic containers vary so greatly, it is important to test the container. When you place it on a surface, observe whether or not the vessel leaks or leaves a ring or mark behind. If the container is not completely waterproof, then you have several options: you can line it with a strong floral plastic, paint the inside of the container with a sealant (allowing appropriate time to dry, and for perhaps a second coat), or use a slightly smaller waterproof "insert" container for water.

AMERICAN ART POTTERY: A NATURAL ZEN CHOICE

Many containers handcrafted in America during what is called the Craftsman period—
an artistic revolution that took place from the mid-1890s to about 1923—are simple,
elegant, and organic. For both architecture and home accessories, artists of the
Craftsman period held an appreciation for more simple forms and more natural,
muted materials. Their goal was to inspire serenity and help people connect with
nature and their surroundings.

As such, Craftsman art pottery is a natural choice for Zen arrangements. Refined,
in matte shades of green, blue, mauve, brown, and mustard, a number of these
pieces—from Teco, Grubey, Weller, Roseville, Artus Van Briggle, and Bauer—utilize
glazes and motifs inspired by Asian cultures. Artus Van Briggle, an artist, mold maker,
and model maker, borrowed from his love of fourth-century Chinese Ming Dynasty art
pottery and the matte glazes of it (used from 960 to 1500) to develop his U.S.-made
pottery. He traveled to Europe and to Asia in search of creating the velvety softness
of the Asian pottery, determined to recreate the "lost art" in his establishment of Van
Briggle Pottery in Colorado Springs in 1899.

The Bauer Pottery Company (1885–1962), in particular, used iron-rich, red-burn-
ing clay mined in Santa Monica, California, which they then formed by machine into
unglazed flower pots. In the kiln, both body and glaze matured simultaneously, result-
ing in a deep matte finish, sometimes porous and sometimes pitted. Improvements in
the firing process resulted in tighter, more opaque matte greens, blues, and browns,
producing an almost silky finish, although not resistant to imperfections. This look was
succeeded by a lustrous blend of green glaze, somewhat transparent, with iridescent
highlights. The classic shapes and motifs, such as some of the ones shown here,
work equally well with just a few select stems or a more full-bodied arrangement.

GLASS: Glass is a clear, clean element. The visibility of the pure water through it represents energy. Glass is advantageous because it can be very inexpensive, is readily available, and is oftentimes a chameleon that can work in many spaces with various presentations. Glass is crisp, modern, and refreshing. The advantage of working with clear glass is the ability to observe the stem(s) and flowers, as well as every element placed under water. This works well for calla lilies or tulips, where the elegant sweep of the stems can greatly enhance one's design. These types of flowers are clean and do not cloud the water much, thus allowing it to remain beautifully clear for several days. A clear vase also works well to showcase an intertwined bundle of underwater willow. Colored, tinted, or distressed glass provides a beautiful texture in which to design.

In order to evoke a warm feeling with glass, avoid angular or cylindrical shapes. Instead, lean toward rounder, more full-bodied shapes—or ornate glass vases—with intricate detailing, such as handblown or etched glass. Investing in a superb vessel by a designer or manufacturer such as Lalique, Tiffany, or Cartier will make a significant contribution to your Zen floral design.

STONE: The solid mineral matter of which rock is made suggests strength and power. Stone can be either warm or cool. Vessels crafted from stone are especially suited for a Zen-style arrange-

ment because of their purely organic nature. Combined with a delicate stem of flora, stone represents the concept of harmonious balance and the merging of textures yin and yang.

The look of natural stone can be very appealing and oftentimes grounds and supports the design while almost fading into the background. A tall, narrow stone vase is perfect for housing a tall cymbidium stem because of its shape and because the weight of the stone will securely hold the weight of the stem, which has a heavier flower. The color of natural stone works tonally with almost any flower color or décor, and natural stone can be very attractive even while sitting empty. A stone vessel also works well with a flower frog. Some stone is porous and can leak, so check for this before completing the design. If your stone vessel leaks, line the interior with heavy plastic sheeting or use an insert container.

TERRA-COTTA: From the earth, both traditional and contemporary terra-cotta can be used to hold arrangements of Zen flowers effectively and in a variety of ways. All terra-cotta pots should be lined with plastic, and floral foam and papier-mâché inserts often work well in these vessels. This technique allows for precise arrangement of the flowers, as once they are embedded in the wet foam and kept still, they will flourish. Foam should be replenished with fresh water every day to prevent drying. Alternatively, place a small jar inside the terra-cotta pot and arrange in the jar.

WOOD: Be it bamboo, reed, or bark, the textures, colors, and types of wood available are varied and unique. From dramatic, dark mahogany and walnut to the palest oak, pine, and birch, wood is often the perfect choice. The natural harmony of wood with most flora is a reflection of true nature, connected eternally and mystically.

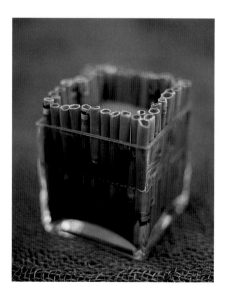

Wood is a beautiful choice for a warm, natural style. It can also be very modern, with sleek lines. One of the drawbacks is that many wood containers are not designed to hold water. This can be solved by using water tubes for smaller blossoms or, for larger blooms, a glass or ceramic container placed inside the wooden vessel. If set deep enough, this dropped-in container will not show; however, if necessary, it can easily be camouflaged with a few bits of moss or a few well-appointed leaves. Depending on how the wooden vase or bowl of wood is crafted—it can be elegant or funky— keep in mind that the container should never overwhelm the flowers and make the arrangement seem "bottom heavy."

WICKER AND OTHER BASKET MATERIALS: Basket weaving is an ancient cultural art form that spans the globe. Baskets can be breathtaking when worked into a Zen arrangement appropriately. Bamboo, woven bark, and grass-reed baskets from Asia—particularly China, Thailand, and Korea—offer a myriad of options for your Zen design. In the United States, the Amish of Pennsylvania and the Southern artisans of Louisiana and the Carolinas, where mosses and lichen grow abundantly, offer beautiful designs rich in detail.

Because of the materials used in their creation, baskets and wickers impart a very strong natural texture. One can pick up on this texture and carry it over into a design, replicating the tones, shape, and nature of the raw materials into the arrangement. Bear in mind, however, that baskets appear bulkier than vases; take this fact into account when choosing your basket, and design in proportion to your botanicals.

Before you begin working with a basket of any kind, seek out a well-made, sturdy, beautiful basket that stands on its

own. It must be a quality basket to sustain a Zen arrangement. Next, be sure to line it thoroughly with plastic and either use floral foam or an insert container to hold your blooms. Since it may be hard to replenish or change the water, design with hearty flowers such as orchids, proteas, and tropicals, which last once in place.

CHOOSING YOUR VESSEL: QUESTIONS TO ASK YOURSELF

The proper container is essential. With all these options available, how does one begin to assess them and find the perfect vessel? The selection process may be approached from several perspectives, depending upon whether one has a vase that typically inhabits a particular space in the home or one is about to purchase a container for a special arrangement.

Taking into account the purpose of the arrangement and the intended effect, begin by asking yourself the following questions:

1. Will the look of the container work for the space and florals I plan on using?

2. Will the container hold adequate water for the life of the blossoms? (If the arrangement is for a party or function this may not be as important.)

3. Will the flowers be in proportion to the container size?

4. Will the flowers and the vessel complement each other, or will they compete?

5. Will the size of the overall presentation be appealing for the space it is to be placed in?

Notice that these questions combine two qualities of Zen: *aesthetics* and *practicality*. First, the overall style of the container must "work" for both the blooms and the environment in which the vessel is placed. It must function practically—that is, hold enough water and have a wide enough opening to accommodate the flowers. The flowers must work in proportion to the vase, so both the size and the shape, or aesthetics, of the vessel are key. Finally, the overall vessel and its finish must not compete with the flowers. This balance is the life force of the arrangement.

When one finds the appropriate container, one is halfway home to creating a perfect arrangement; so, never hurry this part of the process. Begin by stepping back and studying the empty vessel. Assess its possibilities and limitations. Pay attention to its size and shape, and envision the types of materials needed to make the arrangement successful. The end goal is to create energy and beauty, and to be able to visualize the flowers and their vessel in ultimate harmony.

As you experiment, the key is to notice *how you feel* when you place the flowers in the container.

SIZE: When assessing the size of the vessel, trust your eye. Does the vessel look too small or too big to accommodate the flower? How big is the mouth? Is there only enough of an opening for one single, exquisite stem? If you were to place the flower or flowers in the vase, would it tip over? Would the vessel consume the flowers? Does it work on the intended surface (such as the corner table or the breakfast nook); does it seem either too big or too small for the intended space?

PROPORTION AND BALANCE: Related to size are issues of proportion and balance. Assessing the proportion of the vase to the flower(s) should be almost instinctual. An important consideration is for the flowers not to dwarf the vessel, and vice versa. The flower stems must feel supported and in perfect alignment with the vessel of choice. If the stems intentionally droop over the rim of the container, if the stems don't emerge from the mouth correctly, or if the flowers themselves are having a difficult time coming into alignment, then likely the choice of vessel is incorrect.

When working with proportion, a good rule of thumb is one-third vase and two-thirds flowers in vertical height for a tall display. A short, squat arrangement is a bit different: The height of the container and height of the flowers may be the same, but the massed flowers could "visually outweigh" that of the vessel. Therefore, select a vase that has the same approximate "visual weight" as the flowers.

SHAPE: A tall and slender vessel can be very effective for flowers that wish to retain their length, such as grasses, reeds, Asiatic

lilies, long-stemmed tulips, agapanthus, ornithogalum, montbretia, tuberoses, larkspur, blossomwood, and peonies.

Containers with large openings lend themselves to either a mass of flowers or a squat arrangement, as they tend to have a lot of weight to them. Low, shallow dishes are perfect to float a blossom solo, perhaps with an added stone or handsome piece of wood or foliage to create the effect of a reflection or meditative pool. This same low dish type is also perfect when used in conjunction with a flower frog to create a classic "Zen" arrangement featuring a sparse presentation with a few well-chosen blossoms and twigs.

Besides these and a dozen other options, the following tried-and-true shapes will keep you well equipped for just about any design:

Cubes and rectangles: A Flower Box favorite is the cube. Cubes are available in a variety of sizes, from 1-inch square to 24-inches square and larger. Cubes are perfect for creating a contemporary look. A striking centerpiece can be created by combining multiple, same-sized cubes, or by combining multiple cubes of different sizes or alternating heights, such as the alternating sizes in the centerpiece shown here.

Cylinders: Like rectilinear forms, cylinders offer a variety of design options. Tall and thin or short and squat, cylinders vary in height from 3 inches to 5 feet tall. They too may be combined in a variety of ways for a striking centerpiece—particularly if

the design choice is to repeat the same-shape vase but in varying heights. Cylinders are especially useful for the "spillover" effect —that is, if you can't combine all the flowers you'd like to use in one vase, you can split them up among two or three cylinders.

Ceramic bowls: While most people think of a bowl as round, bowls are designed in a plethora of shapes, from round and oblong to square and rectangular. The wonderful aspect about designing with bowls is that every angle works. The key to working with bowls is to make sure the flowers are the right size and length. Because bowls do not have a lip or rim to hold the flower in position, pins or frogs are usually necessary. A weave of crisscrossed twigs can also be used to hold the arrangement in place. It is usually a good idea to use flowers or grasses that do not have heavy stems; this way, the design will look balanced and peaceful.

Some ideas for working with bowls include these arrangements: an oblong black antique ceramic bowl with three gardenias floating upright, or a square bowl showcasing tall, elegant birds of paradise.

In addition to the oblong or geometric bowl, standard round "fishbowls," available in a variety of sizes, work with an array of blooms, including hydrangeas, peonies, roses, lilac, freesia, and daisies. This container can be used to create a very simple modernistic design, by using one type of flower in mass or by skewing the flowers to one side to create symmetry.

Ceramic and glass jars: The ceramic jar, a container available in a variety of shapes, is usually quite squat in appearance and rounded, with a large flat base. The rim of the jar varies in size depending on the purpose of the jar, whether it was made to store grain, water, tea, or incense. Its purpose determines the size and style of the jar lip; however, the lip of the jar is always smaller than the base and circumference. Each jar will have its own unique color(s) and glaze(s). Some jars have lids, which can be removed and displayed next to the jar as part of the overall design.

In many ways, the ginger jar is an easy Zen design choice, especially when

you are working with longer-stemmed flowers or a variety of blooms. This classic shape has a wide bottom to hold all of the flower stems, which allows them to drink heartily. At the same time, the smaller-proportioned "neck" of the vase gives the stems the kind of support they need. Upright flowers that need to be placed at an angle or "fanned out"—such as roses—flourish in ginger jars.

DESTINATION: The placement of your arrangement and its environment is the focus of the next chapter. When choosing your vessel, it is necessary to consider its ultimate destination. Although the selected vessel may be perfect for the blooms on hand, and although one may have created an effective and beautiful design *in and of itself*, one must bear in mind the vessel's ultimate home. Consider the background and foreground of your design and the surface itself, and determine whether or not your vessel works in the intended area. Step back and observe. If the vase is simply too big or too small, too ornate or simple, or doesn't evoke the right emotional response, consider working with a different container.

BRINGING IT ALL TOGETHER

Balance, being the key to happiness and health in life, is crucial to the designs one

creates, as this will convey a sense of well-being and peace in the home or office.

As you work on bringing together your flowers in their vessels, allow the natural lines of the flowers to come through, maintaining a sense of movement and freedom. Although your tendency might be to bind and contort flowers and foliage into stylized arrangements, this more formal structured style of design may not give you the freedom to impart a sense of Zen beauty and nature into your space. Attune yourself to the natural flow of the arrangement by simply observing the shapes of the flowers and foliage or twigs, and by observing how those relate to your vessel of choice.

FINISHING TOUCHES: Consider the power of the leaf and stem. How might integrating, wrapping, or otherwise working with stems and leaves add a finishing touch to your vessel? When working with glass, try lining the inside of the vase with something to add color and interest, such as wrapping a large leaf around the inside of the vase or filling it with fruit. Key here is limiting the number of elements. Whenever you add an additional element—be it a swath of fabric or a handful of bear grass or willow—keep it simple and organic. Never cross the line into something that seems too distorted or at odds with natural form.

ENVIRONMENT

A flowerless room is a soulless room,
to my way of thinking; but even one solitary little vase of a living flower may redeem it.
—Vita Sackville-West

*Flowers magically transform an environ-*ment. Rooms filled with flowers are infused with energy and vitality. Homes welcome the inclusion of handpicked arrangements and work environments spark creativity with the touch of a well-appointed stem. Almost any room can be enhanced with the placement of fresh flowers or greens. By shifting the energy of a room, enlightening the space, and stimulating your surroundings, one inherently offers a glimpse of calm and a feeling of peace to all who enter.

With a little experimentation, it's possible to achieve widely diverse effects in the same environment, whether one is working with a full arrangement or the accent of a single flower. The same space can host an exuberant celebration, welcome a quiet dinner with loved ones, function as a practical workspace, or become a meditative sanctuary—depending upon the floral touch. How many of us have used our dining-room tables or bedroom nightstand for multiple purposes?

Consider the purpose of the event, the occasion it celebrates, the season it evokes, and the feelings you are inviting; make an effort to engage both psyche and soul. No matter what the end design, one fact is certain: When you take in the energy from the materials you are working with and impart yours back, you will create a marvelous synergy that will mystically and beautifully lift any space. By trusting your instincts and remaining open to change as you assemble your flowers, you almost guarantee that any space will sing.

vigor." Consider the effect that flowers will have on people exposed to them. Be sensitive to the emotions of those who will encounter the arrangement.

One dear friend of ours loved her weekly arrangement so much that, although it was intended for a particular spot in her home, she would pick it up and carry it with her from room to room. "I can't explain what it is about this particular arrangement. Maybe it's the life and love that you pour into it. But I can't help but notice how it makes me feel, so it sits with me when I dine, when I work, and when I sleep. No matter where I venture in my home, there it is beside me."

GETTING TO KNOW YOUR SPACE

The desire for peace and tranquility in our environment is a quest we all embark on at some point in our lives. The Zen concept of this quest is to balance simplicity and serenity, while observing a keen sense of beauty in a space for living and working. We can apply the Zen design to all our surroundings, little by little, step by step. The essential process is one that rids our environment of clutter, creates light and space, and embraces and fills the void with lines, shades, hues, and colors, leaving room for beautiful, simple objects of art and, in this case, the Zen floral design.

Before designing a Zen arrangement, one must get to know the "space." This may be a corner of your kitchen, a big, open living-room table, or multiple place-

EVOKING EMOTION

The most important aspect of placing florals inside or outside the home, workspace, or event site is deciding what type of feeling one is trying to create. Every arrangement begins with the evoking of emotion, and it's essential to get in touch with the emotions one is trying to impart. The process involves taking a moment to step back and consider how a particular flower makes one feel. Does its color please you? Will the fragrance add to the ambiance of the room or be overwhelming? What does the space seem to be calling for? Perhaps you need a flash of color—a hot accent to enliven and "pop" the room. Or would you like to convey a calming, meditative feeling?

Henry Ward Beecher once said, "Flowers have a mysterious and subtle influence upon the feelings, not unlike some strains of music. They relax the tenseness of the mind. They dissolve its

FLORAL "SCENTSIBILITY"

The olfactory nerves are the only ones that connect directly to the brain. No wonder fragrances have such a profound effect on the human psyche. Many people who have wandered into The Flower Box over the years have remarked about their emotional connections to a particular flower. "My grandmother used to grow peonies." "My grandfather was the one who introduced me to his rose garden." "My wife loves the smell of lavender!" We all have sentimental, emotional, primal, instinctual, learned, and heartfelt responses to the beauty and energy of flowers' fragrances and essences. The mere suggestion of our favorite fragrance can bring a smile to our lips or open up our mind to new thoughts. It can bring a tear to our eye or remind us of romance long since gone; it can make us feel a certain way as we remember events from the past or envision plans for the future. A flower can do all this instantly, simply by being.

settings at a formal event. It may be one's home, home office, or a 2,500-square-foot loft.

Ponder the following generalities as you begin:

CONSIDER THE EVENT: For what reason are you placing the flowers? Is it time for celebration? Is it the first day of spring? Are you having a warm family dinner, or anticipating a recuperative weekend at home? Do you wish to create a spa-like sanctuary in your bathroom? How about a festive burst for your kitchen?

SURVEY THE ROOM: Before you put flower to vessel, stand quietly in the center of your space. Close your eyes for a few moments and take in the colors, the vibrancy or subtlety of their hues, the scents, and the décor. What might glorify the room and welcome you and your guests? At The Flower Box, we often place different colors, shapes, and sizes of arrangements within the same room just to see what their effect is on the room itself. Many times we are surprised by the effect a particular shade of green or blue will have on a space, and end up changing our plan midcourse. While this may not

be practical for a home setting, the lesson remains the same: You need to see the arrangement within the environment in order to achieve your desired result.

Absorb the shapes and sizes of *all* the components of the room. Are you trying to highlight and brighten or bring attention to a space, or would a better alternative be to use calming, soothing colors—similar colors to those of the room? What size flowers might be consistent in the space? Would a contrast be more effective? Sometimes, in a very large room, we use masses of the same kind of small flower or simply two or three stems of a very large-headed blossom. Another alternative in this same large room, especially if it boasts large, expansive furniture, is to snip a piece of a beautiful tree—perhaps blossom wood or the new growth of leaves for the season in a fresh, clean, bright green.

NOTICE THE DETAILS: A room's architecture, lighting, and décor are factors that contribute to the arrangement you ultimately select, so it's important to take a snapshot of these elements in your mind and revisit them as you arrange. Take into consideration textures and textiles. Are you

VIEW YOUR AREA AS A CANVAS. How will a theatrical splash of color, a single bud, a few leaves of grass in a tall glass cylinder draw attention to a piece of art or accent a space? Engage in freedom, draw on your senses, and develop an eye for beauty in unexpected places. Imagine an elegant water lily, bouncing from a dark surface, bringing life and energy to a corner of the room—a small touch of beauty that gives one immediate pleasure.

in an environment of antiques, do you have a mingling of contemporary and traditional? Observe the wood of your furniture; is it a dark, rich walnut or mahogany or a clean pine? Or do you have modernistic elements of marble, granite, and steel? Do you have wooden floors, throw rugs, or carpeting? Do you have many *objets d'art* or a few knick-knacks? Are the art pieces demanding and colorful, subtle and restful, or both? These considerations will help you decide what kind of accent your floral design should be. Zen can be large or small, happy or serene, but should always complement the room.

FREE UP YOUR SPACE: The sheer amount of furniture and artwork within the environment makes a statement all its own. Don't be afraid to lean more toward the minimalist, put unnecessary things away, leave as little as possible, to be functional and charming. Let the space gain momentum by allowing for clean, uncluttered surfaces on which to place your design.

SACRED SPACES, SPECIAL SANCTUARIES

Throughout the world and throughout time, human beings have created sacred sanctuaries—clean, uncluttered spaces of retreat to explore the mind. Places to leave the world of the mundane and explore the world of the spiritual and uplifting. Sanctuaries are those places in which we seek solace.

Many cultures embrace the realization that a feeling of well-being is as important as being physically healthy. A space to explore the mind and tap into one's inner life force has motivated people to build places of quiet from the smallest home altar to wonderful masterpieces of architectural design. More than a specific living space, a sanctuary is a space where human dimension and spirituality harmonize, becoming our own private paradise. A sanctuary is our own private world within a larger universe, where we keep the world at arm's reach and retreat into the tranquility of our special space.

Few people realize that one's home, or living space, provides ample opportunity

for such a sacred space, and that it does not take a Herculean effort to transform one's home into one's sanctuary. The challenge lies in appreciating the space one has and learning to work with it.

Making a sacred space can be as simple as setting up a corner of a room with a mat facing east, with no clutter and a small table. Many people who meditate, pray, or practice yoga on a regular basis dedicate a special space to seeking serenity. One might also create a more elaborate sacred space, exploring an entire room for this purpose.

Often, our sacred spaces involve home altars. The home altar is as unique and significant as the religion it represents. The goal in creating an altar is to tap into humanity's dream of life: to be in mystical harmony with our environment and all of nature. The home altar takes on a deeply personal meaning. In many cultures and religions, especially Buddhism, altars in the home are part of a long tradition and essential to peace of mind.

For any sacred space, choose a part of your home that is quiet, with natural daylight, where you would feel confident that a most honored guest would be comfortable and safe. One can create a universe inside an antique cabinet, or within a modern display case.

Many altars are adorned with flowers and greens, fruit, and water—all symbolic of life eternal. People often burn incense to cleanse the air and engage the sense of smell with a beautiful fragrance. Japanese incense is made with dried leaves and has no oil, making it very pure. As such, it leaves no stains or smoke when it burns, keeping the environment clean.

When incorporating a Zen floral design into a home altar, cleanliness is most important. Fresh water and fresh flowers are the keys to adorning this space. The offering can be a simple group of lotus

pods or a mass of white lilies, fragrant and pure. There are no "rules" here; select flowers that work well with the space you've created and that appeal to your personal sensibilities.

Adolf Loos once said, "Your home will be made with you and you with your home." This is true of our spiritual sacred space, the place that involves the melding of the psyche and the soul. In addition, Zen concepts of tranquility and order can be applied to one's entire living space; one may invoke a sense of peace in almost any room of the home.

THE HOME:
A ROOM-BY-ROOM EXPLORATION

"I am the space where I am," said the French poet Noel Arnaud. The home is a complex place made up of many components: memories, traditions, hopes, fears, celebrations—both past and present. It encompasses our routines and dreams and is our own multidimensional space. And each of us puts our own touch and energy into each aspect of the space that exists. The comfort of our lifestyle is affected by the order of our home furnishings, the types and amount of light, and the color palettes we select—right down to the single stem.

THE LIVING AREA: Of all our spaces, the living area—the domestic space—is the place where we unwind and put our feet up. The living area is just that: *the place where we live*, not necessarily a designated space with a purpose for eating, sleeping, or bathing, but our own room to explore and expand our creative spirit—or to unwind, relax, and set our minds free of clutter. This area is usually defined by comfortable seating arrangements, sofas and armchairs, tables of wood, marble, and glass, each

with its own individuality. This space also houses our collected treasures, works of art, and books. And more often than not, it doubles as a workspace.

One of the most important features of our living room is the atmosphere determined by the lighting we have chosen. The lighting of the room might be derived from lamps and warm lampshades, or perhaps a modern strip of recessed lighting, each chosen according to one's specific taste in a desire to enter an area that is a haven. In Zen design, things of beauty are enhanced by subtle and enriching light. The approach to light can be seen in the East-West marriage of bamboo, silk, and paper lanterns with a not-too-bright lightbulb, providing warmth, atmosphere, and shadows. Allow the mystery of your floral design to unfold and its underlying beauty to be exposed based on where it is placed and how the light catches it. In Zen, the aesthetic is more subtle than obvious, and the floral design should embrace this concept.

When choosing a design of fresh flowers for your living area, consider the areas you would like to enrich or accentuate. Is there a beautiful color in a painting you would like to emphasize? If so, choose the flower(s) with the same color palette, place them in a vessel, and position the design in close proximity to the painting—close enough to make the connection but not to clutter the area.

Or consider placing an arrangement of wistful orange poppies or cream mag-

nolias next to a beautiful lamp that illuminates the surrounding area and adds ambiance to the room.

The use of shiny gold persimmons on an ornate plate placed on a dark wooden surface transforms a dead space to one of abundance and life. Incorporating bamboo into your design introduces a simple Zen effect. With its many uses and textures, bamboo offers a clean, simple appeal. It summarizes the influence of Zen versatility.

Make a bold, striking Zen statement with an oversized ceramic or stone vessel. Place this in an area where the light casts shadows and hues. Try arranging Casablanca lilies in the vessel. Dubbed "the queen of lilies," these are rich with fragrance. Although they are expensive, their long life span makes them worth the expense. (Remember this professional tip: Remove the stamens as soon as the bud starts to open. This prevents the orange dust from staining the flower and surrounding surfaces.)

When working with floral arrangements, the key is to consider the relationship between flowers and their vessel and the furniture the arrangement will be placed on. Always consider the mood you are trying to create. Thoughtful visual presentations offer endless possibilities for bringing to life the neglected corner, the bare table, or the abandoned shelf.

Try the following flowers in your living room to evoke freshness and love: Magnolias, Cymbidium orchids, hydrangea, French tulips, gerbera daisies, hyacinths, lilac, apple and pear blossoms, iris, gladiolus, peonies, columbine, chrysanthemum, dahlia, lotus pods.

THE DINING SPACE: The dining table is the heart of the home in all cultures. It's where friends and family gather to celebrate, to eat and drink, to talk and laugh, to entertain and delve into the innermost aspects of their lives. It's the place for simple family meals and the setting of many special occasions and traditions.

When arranging your floral design, consider the space you have to work with, the shape of your table and chairs, the colors of the room, and the amount of lighting available. Consider, too, the practical details of linens, napkin holders, and tableware. What is the ambiance of your dining room? Is it clean and practical? Infused with warmth and an inviting atmosphere? Or a bit of both? Since this area is usually host to many colors and textures of food and drink, it requires the simplest Zen flower arrangement. For the dining-room table, usually less is more. Need we mention that the flowers should be fresh and the water clean? Another must is that the flowers' scents are minimal, so that they don't compete with the smell of the food served.

Consider too the flow of the *chi* (energy) in the room, and the ease with which people can move around the table when food is served or excusing them-

SEASONS CHANGE

The dining and living areas provide wonderful opportunities for reflecting and complementing the changing cuisine of the seasons. Spring blossoms include hyacinth, tulips, and roses—all in abundance during the warmer months. These flowers make lovely accents to crisp, white linens and dreamy creams. Autumn provides gourds, squashes, pumpkins, and branches of flaming red and bold orange maple and oak leaves. Winter is abundant with burnt orange, shades of gold, reds, purples, and burgundies, and rich green colors. Holly, pine, and narcissus all say "holiday" and ring in the New Year.

selves. The dining-table arrangement should complement this, and not be overpowering. Key is that the arrangement allows for eye contact and conversation across the table, so low arrangements that don't obstruct one's view are best. Consider gloriosa lilies—which are available in many colors—cut low, with smooth pebbles in an oblong dish—a very striking presentation with contrasting textures.

Laurel leaves, known as sweet bay, a simple edible foliage, works well when cut low and placed in several clear glass square vessels along the center of the table. Alternatively, one can place a tall iris or gladioli arrangement in a stone or ceramic vessel in a nearby serving area, in which case an arrangement on the dining table itself is not necessary.

Dining is itself a celebration of life. Invite life into the room by placing well-appointed stems in more than one locale. A bonsai tree placed near a window can invite a Zen feel to the room. Bonsai can thrive for years with the correct care and attention, and bring an element of nature into the room. Similarly, orchids bring a simple, clean look to almost any dining space.

Try the following flowers in your dining room, to complement—not compete with—the aromas of food: Golden yew, orchids, delphinium, Lenten roses, snowberries, Easter lilies, stargazer lilies, miniature persimmons, Japanese camellias, anemones, floating cosmos, crow gourds.

THE BEDROOM: Of all the rooms in the home, the bedroom embodies both the *yin* space—where we enjoy quiet, privacy, tranquility, relaxation, and stillness—and the *yang* space, where we engage in movement, activity, and the powerful life force of sexual activity.

There is a place in Zen design to engage in a dreamy, sensual, and sexy approach when choosing an arrangement for your bedroom. One evocative place to have flowers is next to the bed, where the head rests. The arrangement will engage your senses of smell and sight. It is calming to regard a beautiful flower before closing one's eyes to sleep, its fragrance filtering into your dreamlife.

With your arrangement, you can purposely create a mood that is in harmony with the décor of the bedroom. Observe the colors and ambiance of the room. Is it whimsical and feminine, or bold and masculine? Invoke sensuality by experimenting with fragrant white gardenias, whose dark green leaves, floating in a stone dish of fresh water, will bring a beautiful, restful appearance with a strong sensual fragrance. Alternatively, a tall, clean glass cylinder of long-stemmed mint green hydrangea or black cala lilies will appeal to a masculine sensibility. For a bold, sexy arrangement, select tall gold or brown cymbidium orchids. Just one stem will add warmth and a glow to an otherwise dead corner. These are long-lasting flowers and are beautiful in a simple wooden vessel, harmonizing with the wood in the

room, blending with the fabrics and textiles. In the few weeks of the year they make their appearance, peonies—white, coral, sultry dark, and the palest pinks—are a must, particularly in the bedroom. Select one, cut it short, and place it in a short, simple vase. Watch the tiny bud open up to become a huge bloom of magnificent and fragrant silky petals.

Lady slippers, cut or growing, ooze mystery. They are available in various sultry colors: pastel lemons, dark rich mahogany, and plum tones. Chocolate cosmos in a square glass vase is another exciting bedroom flower, with its dark brown petals and fragrance of dark chocolate; a mass of these leaning to one side in just the right vessel is strong and charming.

Flowers need light, so although the bedroom will be dark and peaceful at night, in the day it should offer a light and breezy atmosphere in order for the arrangement to thrive.

Don't hesitate to adorn your resting space with two or three separate styles of flowers; think of nature and its abundance of styles and scents. Or consider one lone orchid, placed in a water tube, strategically positioned on your lover's pillow; a handpicked daisy, with a special note, placed on your daughter's nightstand.

Try the following flowers in your bedroom to welcome peace and tranquility: calla lilies, orchids, lady slippers, gardenia, peonies, lily of the valley, Casablanca lilies, honeysuckle, jasmine, roses.

THE BATHROOM: The bathroom—abundant with various flows of running water—is a cleansing, healing, spiritual environment. It has the ability to simultaneously offer the feelings of invigoration, freshness, health, calmness, and relaxation. Soft textures of linens and towels are often complemented by cooler textures of enamel, marble, tile, steel, and glass.

Almost any bathroom can benefit from a simple, clean arrangement. One, three, or five tall white or purple iris speak of tranquility and elegance, the green stems and delicate flowers displaying their clean, simple lines. Iris work best when placed in a tall glass vase, so that their stems are in full view.

Imagine three distinct black calla lilies. Elegant and striking, they can balance the clean, hard lines of a cold bathroom with their gentleness. Two apple green anthurium, cut at different levels, secured by a frog, and placed in a small round container, make an arrangement that is both simple and wildly unique.

Alternatively, fragrant flowers bring abundant energy, healing, and warmth. Branches of fresh orange blossom invigorate. A mass of blue, cream, or white hyacinth soothes the soul, and tall tuberose, with its late-afternoon seductive spray of perfume, lends a strong tropical aroma to the batch. Try utilizing vessels that are simple and unobtrusive, and that blend with the coolness of the room. The flowers will speak volumes in such a sparse space. Let them.

Orchid plants, with their exotic blooms, graceful, arching stems, and rich dark green leaves thrive in well-lit and humid spaces, often making them the perfect choice for the bathroom.

The bathtub and basin are great places to experiment with bud vases and floral tubes. When combined with candles and incense, flowers can transform a bathroom into a soothing space, free from the stresses of the day.

Try the following scents in your bathroom to invite a spa-like atmosphere: eucalyptus, lavender, lime, lemongrass, tuberose, narcissus, bamboo, bear grass, succulents of all types, freesia, orchids, ginger, anthurium, cockscomb, hyacinth bulbs.

THE KITCHEN: The culinary space may be a small corner or a busy environment with many surfaces to consider. Before you get started on your design, eliminate the clutter and hide the unappealing. Move cleaning products out of sight, and store as much as possible in cupboards. Try to have as little as possible sitting out on the counter to distract the eye. If it is not your style to have a Zen kitchen, ensure that the Zen flower arrangement becomes the focal point of the room.

Choose grasses, lavenders, reeds, blossoms, and succulents, flowers and plants that can withstand changing temperatures, especially heat. Because kitchens are not fragile spaces, the vessels used should be sturdy and practical.

Tall branches of spring blossoms—be they lemon, apple, pear, or cherry—dogwood branches, laurel leaves, or a huge bunch of lilacs, are wonderful additions for any kitchen. Each can be arranged in a large stone vase, and will add a majestic touch to a very domestic environment. In autumn, persimmon, bittersweet, squash, and gourds placed in the stone vases offer a warmer, comforting element.

A low, rectangular ceramic dish of fresh, green succulents near a window invariably adds life and energy. A mass of ruby-red French tulips or a bunch of bright orange parrot tulips in a terra-cotta vessel makes a bold statement in any busy environment. Fresh lavender and growing herbs, such as tarragon, rosemary, chives, and basil, invite the outdoor environment

inside. They play a double role as the perfect food enhancers, easily snipped with a pair of kitchen scissors for inclusion in your favorite herb sack. Dried linseed stems with golden tones warm up the coldest kitchen space; place them in an iron or copper jug on a wide workspace.

The kitchen is both a place of nurturing and gathering. The "busy-ness" of the kitchen ignites more energy than perhaps any other room, and it is frequently filled with activity, from baking to homework to pots of Earl Grey tea. Because of the energy here, you can be much more flamboyant with your design. As in all aspects of Zen, don't clutter, but be selective and brave.

Try the following flowers in your kitchen to complement the fragrances and flavors of cuisine: Chinese lanterns, orange and lemon blossoms, heather, laurel, rosemary, dill, pepper, parrot tulips, gentians, primrose, pansies, poppies, bittersweet, sweet pea.

THE WORKSPACE—BRINGING JOY INTO DAILY ROUTINE: The workspace is the one area where clutter seems to build, particularly on one's desk or primary work surface. It is also the space where we allow our minds to wander through a million creative thoughts and images. Keeping one's workspace organized and functional is an almost eternal quest. In this sense our creativity is like seeds that are scattered by the wind or flying insects; they land, take root, complete their journey

on earth by producing flowers and fruits, trees, and grasses. Each seed begins its journey to fruition out of a certain amount of precarious, necessary chaos. And so it is with our creativity.

In our culture of noise and sensationalism, a sense of calm and peace within our workspace is essential. Be the creator of your own workspace cocoon by allowing for different levels of intensity and personality on your desk, near your computer, on bookshelves. Depending upon what you do for a living and the amount of space you have to work with, a variety of Zen floral designs could work here. Remember, simple is usually best, and that by simply introducing life into your workspace you will inspire creativity.

It is always a good idea to keep water away from the workspace, for practical reasons. An arrangement situated *near* a phone or computer, rather than right *next* to it, works best. If you long to have a floral design on your desk, try experimenting with water tubes, so that the water is contained and cannot spill onto precious paperwork. You can also move tubed flowers around at random, dotting your desk and file cabinets on a creative whim. When working with water tubes, choose a flower with a strong stem, such as an apple or cherry blossom, a single gerbera daisy, an agapanthus stem, or thistle, all of which are long lasting and sturdy.

For a stationary arrangement, a beautiful orchid plant is ideal. Some prefer the single stem of an orchid flower, as watching the process of the flower buds opening one by one is symbolic of the completion of a project, step by step—be it paying the bills or creating the next masterpiece. Savor the extraordinary meltonia, the unique wilsonaria—both exotic, long lasting, and inspirational "wildcat" orchids.

Grasses and greens represent eternal life. Stalks of bamboo, a frond of sword fern, fig branches, or stalks of bear grass bring a calming energy to the creative space. These can be placed in a minimum amount of water in a shallow bowl or heavy jar (that won't easily be knocked over) and secured with the use of pins (frogs).

Try the following scents in your workspace to inspire creativity: eucalyptus, daisies, freesia, orchids, grasses, poppy seed heads, chocolate cosmos, pussy willow.

COLOR, SHAPE & TEXTURE

Colors, like features, follow the change of emotions.   —Pablo Picasso

The four cornerstones of life—color, shape, and texture—are inextricably woven into Zen floral design. To consider one aspect of the flower is to consider all. In order to effectively arouse the observer's imagination and engage the senses, the color, shape, and texture of an arrangement's flowers must all work together as a whole. As such, it is important to consider the color and shape of the flowers as they stand alone, their color and shape in relation to the vessel and environment, and the textured tapestry beautifully inherent in every flower. *Wabi sabi* is Japanese for "wisdom in natural simplicity." This natural simplicity finds its way into every Zen floral design as freedom of expression takes precedence over classic rules.

The neutrality and stillness of a white wall allows the simplest or most complex Zen arrangement to shine.

ZEN ESSENTIALS

Typically, a monochromatic color scheme is the standard background in a Zen room. Monochromatic color harmony suggests contemplation and allows the aspects of a flower's shape and texture to make a statement, arousing emotion when viewed. Often shades of greens and browns, reflecting nature, or whites and creams, representing tranquility, are choice color themes for Zen interiors. Think of the greens in bamboo, which is symbolic of longevity as well as humility and fidelity. The stem is hollow inside and straight outside and it bends in a storm but never breaks. Because Western homes often embrace an entire spectrum of color, it can be more of a challenge to introduce a floral arrangement without cluttering the existing variety of color. *Yang* energy is light, bright, and warm, and evokes movement and activity. *Yin* is cooler, bringing forth concepts of stillness, darkness, passiveness, and water. Consider these two concepts when creating your Zen corners.

Gérard de Nerval said, "Each flower is a soul opening to nature." The single lily bud, bursting with potential, offers the slightest hint of what may be inside. Anticipate the beauty of this bud. It will gradually open to take in the warmth of its environment. A singular bud represents the oneness of spirit and body, the inseparability of nature and the universe. The rich, deep claret color of this Sumatra Asiatic lily is unique in its own right.

A cluster of buds protruding from the same source reaches to the heavens. The waiting for a bud to gently open is as wonderful as the anticipation of a loved one's arrival. The gentle lines of the bud, the sharp points of the leaves, and the strong, sturdy stem offer a unique vision of color, shape, and texture. In a high-gloss black vase, brown urn, or clear glass cylinder, these lilies manifest brightness.

YIN AND YANG PERCEPTION

Like the concept of *yin* and *yang*, every flower contains both feminine and masculine aspects. If one looks very closely at almost any flower, one can see both soft and hard, both light and dark, both sumptuousness and sparseness. In this sense, a flower's primary emotional appeal belongs to the eye of the beholder. There is no reason why a male observing a delicate mauve Vanda orchid cannot be as stirred as he would by a bold, claret Asiatic lily. Similarly, many females find the masculinity of the lotus pod as emotionally enticing as a white Casablanca lily or delicate quince blossom. Zen design challenges preconceived notions of the flower and its ability to communicate more readily to one gender or another.

When the transformation from bud to open flower is complete, one appreciates the contrast of *yin* and *yang* in a single flower. The bold, beautiful arrangement encases an inner world of velvet-smooth tongue-shaped petals, offering a fresh breath of possibility for any room. The large mass of a singular color is a very daring design. The clear, green stems are visible in the glass vessel, adding another dimension to the arrangement as they drink their life-giving water. This arrangement's glorious scent, released when fully open, makes it especially appealing to a living area or bedroom.

VIBRANT YELLOWS, RICH REDS, AND DEEP ORANGES

A mass of color makes a design statement all its own. Whether seven or twenty-seven flowers, there is something about the density of singular color that simultaneously shocks and soothes the senses. It seems particularly fitting that the tulip—the rage of floral design for centuries—is selected to exhibit this concept. Priceless Delft Dutch porcelain was designed specifically to house and show the myriad of tulip types—at one time considered exotic flowers—that became a fad throughout Europe in the sixteenth century. The tulip, one of the most versatile flowers, can be arranged without any difficulty in a variety of styles. One tulip in a vase or vessel can be as striking and awesome as a multitude. And often the stem of a particular tulip can be as interesting as the flower is beautiful.

A singular yellow Monte Carlo tulip rests against cool black slate. Its exquisite shape might be likened to a ballerina, as its curved stem gently stretches forward, arms of leaves reaching toward the slightly opened bud.

The numeral 7 is said to represent the ability of all living creatures to breathe and exist together. A cluster of seven Dutch tulips in a beautiful vessel stand boldly against a rich black marble table. The smooth textures of the vessels and table, all dark and cool, complement the warmth of the yellow tulips. As a final step in this design, we dropped two copper pennies into the vessel; the addition of copper changes the composition of the water and helps the tulip stem stand tall.

A mass of rich reds is breathtaking in this rococo parrot tulip arrangement, which offers a sense of wild abandonment and abundance. The ruffled edge and intricate interior shading found in these tulips' petals is unique to this variety.

The same is true for the arrangement of flaming orange princess tulips, which give the illusion that they are growing out of their ancient Chinese wooden crate. This variety of tulip has double petals, which add to the richness of the design. As the petals open and expand, they deepen in hue and exhibit rich mahogany markings. This coloration further connects them to the color and warmth of the wood.

A SYNTHESIS
OF COLOR, SHAPE, AND TEXTURE

An oblong, clear glass vase with elements of the ocean houses a plethora of monochromatic mauve Vanda orchids. A sumptuous cloud of color emerges from a bed of seashells, and the crisscrossed stems of the flowers add dimension to this Zen arrangement.

SENSUOUS DETAIL

Certain flowers are so rich in color, shape, and texture that they really are like a world in and of themselves. Some discerning onlookers have even noted that flowers like the protea and certain cacti resemble sea anenomes or "outer-space" life forms. The key to the Zen design here is the appreciation and flaunting of this detail; be careful not to overindulge in either the number of flowers used or in an overly ornate vessel, as either choice will detract from the end design.

A king protea is a rich and sensual flower. Originally from the Cape Town area of South Africa, the flower of the king protea can grow to be 12 inches across. The outside of the flower is encased in many stiff, pointed, narrow bracts, or petals, that give it the appearance of a cup. The bottom half of the petals begin as cream colored or yellow, then turn into bright pink or velvet red on the top half. Inside the cup is a soft mass of white stamens about 1 to 2 inches long, which all bend toward the center.

When arranged with quince blossom, the king protea arrangement becomes a study in the contrast of shape and texture. The king protea, powerful and sturdy, is encased by the delicate quince blossom branches and tea tree leaves. Displayed together, these juxtaposing floral textures harmonize beautifully, with color as the binding element. The ancient quince, or *boke no hana* in Japanese, was brought to Japan from Persia during the Heian period. It blossoms in the cold of winter and is used to perfume rooms during this chilling season. It is the symbol of endurance through hardship and of overcoming difficult circumstances. The use of oasis (floral foam) and Spanish moss allow the branches to appear as if from a Zen garden.

The pincushion protea resembles a burst of fireworks, with petals that stretch our conception of what a petal should look like. Its spiky, pine needle-like petals are tinged at the end as if dipped in coral pink ink. The stems are sturdy and ridged and support what appear to some as small universes of exploding stars. Indigenous to South Africa, where it grows on sandstone slopes at high mountain altitudes, the pincushion protea is part of the Cape Floral Kingdom, where it grows only in the winter rainfall area. Pincushion proteas are a good choice for floral arrangements because of their striking appearance and longevity; they appear in a variety of colors, from bright orange to the yellow variety shown here.

Six pincushion proteas seem almost airborne in a crystal vase. Set in a simple glass vase, these flowers practically glow. Note the space between the petals, the space between the stems, and the minimalism of leaves, creating a clean, almost weightless effect.

AMAZING ANTHURIUM

This wildly suggestive bisexual flower offers more than 1,000 species. Its flattened, fleshy heart-shaped petal spreads from the center of a smooth, straight green stem. The free, strong spathe, or stamen, juts from the center of the flower. The flower is extremely variable in form and hue—its colors number in the hundreds, including pure white; rich, chocolate-brown lacquer (aptly called the choco anthurium, shown here); two-tone pink and green; port burgundy; and the palest green inflorescence. The stamens, which present themselves with an unabashed confidence, are just as colorful, offering brilliant reds, bright yellows, even the palest peach pinks. The stamens have a tendency to be smooth and covered with sticky seeds.

The shapes of the obaki anthurium in the highly polished wood vessel are unique and striking, and together make a strong statement. They contrast with the backdrop of an antique Japanese screen made from reeds and bamboo. The flowers are held in place with a florist's frog.

Originally from central and tropical South America, anthurium flowers are abundant throughout the Hawaiian Islands, but few are more unique than the beautiful hybrid choco variety. The inclusion of lotus pods, interlaced with protea greens, presents an interesting study in shape and texture. A handcrafted, glazed ceramic bowl complements the arrangement, allowing the floral design to hold center stage.

DISCREET OR DAZZLING

Although the amaryllis originated in South America's tropical regions, its beautiful large flowers and the ease with which they can be brought to bloom make the flower popular the world over for both growing and harvesting. The amaryllis comes in many colorful varieties, including various shades of red, white, pink, salmon, orange, and stripes. Each stem commonly has four flowers, which usually open one at a time. When the stem reaches maturity and is in full bloom, each flower faces a different direction—East, West, North, and South— a beautiful symbolism of the four directions. Although many perceive this as a strong, masculine flower, the lighter-colored varieties can be very feminine and wistful. Depending upon the color chosen, very different Zen effects can be created with virtually the same arrangement composition. Is the effect you are aiming to create discreet or dazzling? Experimenting with a few stems of this beautiful bulb is sure to bring interesting results.

One peach Minerva amaryllis rests its head against bleached wood. The use of one flower in Zen offers an eye-catching statement. It is not known why odd numbers are more preferable to Zen than even. Suffice it to say that tradition, perception, and religious influence have played a part in embracing odd as opposed to even numbers. A single flower, lying still or in a vase as an arrangement, speaks to the "oneness of life and its environment," an inherently Buddhist concept from Nichiren. The oneness of life draws from nature and offers balance and harmony.

Amaryllis stems make a strong design statement when arranged in three square glass vases, fixed diagonally on this wooden end table. The glass vessel is the perfect choice for this design, as it allows one to view the entirety of the stem. An arrangement like this can transform a shabby-chic corner into a pure Zen feature.

Whether designing with royal velvet
amaryllis (shown here, up close) or the
red lion variety, the bold, hot color
speaks where words cannot.

The en masse arrangement of red lion
amaryllis offers the eye a burst of joy and
energy, and harmonizes with the restful
energy of an entranceway or one's private
sanctuary. Because mirrors reflect light
and can both visually enlarge a space and
redirect the path of energy, they work
well to enhance certain arrangements.
Shown here in full bloom, the amaryllis
starts as a tight bloom and then slowly
opens, exhibiting more color and vibrancy
every day. The longevity of this flower
makes it a perfect choice for a focal point
in one's home.

SPACE

With blossoms

falling

in spaces
between the twigs

a temple
has appeared.

—Buson

The Japanese writer Kenko said, "In everything, no matter what it may be, uniformity is undesirable. Leaving something incomplete makes it interesting, and gives one the feeling that there is room for growth." The Zen flower arrangement avoids symmetry, yet there is a sense of balance; it abhors uniformity, but conveys completeness. In the minimalist spirit, any arrangement prefers the gentle placement of slightly skewed flowers and stems. No two flowers in an arrangement are exactly alike, nor should they be, as those "oddities" found in nature often make the most interesting blooms. While the temptation may be to reserve only the most perfect flowers and stems for an arrangement, try selecting a flower or leaf that looks as if it was freshly plucked from its natural setting. You'll find the arrangement will, almost by default, be free from pretension or self-consciousness and, rather, exude a feeling of spontaneity. The result will be a much more organic presentation.

An aesthetically pleasing integration of all elements—branch, flower, leaf, and vessel—derives from a conscious use of space. Space within the vessel, space between the flowers, even space between the branch, bud, and leaf of a flower, all allow for a living, breathing invention.

The Asian culture has always expressed that one lotus blossom floating in the middle of a clear, still pond offers the viewer a deeper level of inner examination than the overuse of color abundant in many Western arrangements. This liberal use of space, and emphasis on the singular, is key to any arrangement that exudes harmony. Both the way that the flowers are placed within the vessel and the appeal that is created by the inclusion of space illustrate two of the simplest principles of any effective composition. Rather than fill all of the space in the arrangement, the Zen arrangement attempts to reach deeper into our senses by allowing the arrangement *to breathe*.

SIMPLISTIC CYMBIDIUM

For a minimalist effect that suits most every room, one or two cymbidium orchids in a clear glass vase present a stunning effect. Understated yet elegant, orchids are one of the few universally intriguing plants to have stirred humankind's passions. With its exotically beautiful "face," each blossom is unique in shape, color, and texture, making it the perfect flower for design experimentation. Science has created many hybrid varieties, with a color spectrum that boasts bright reds, deep golden browns, burnt oranges, pale pinks, and rich yellows.

The orchid recalls the sensual and exotic, partly because of the flower's sex life, which often involves the drama of desire and deception. The bucket orchid, of genus *Coryanthes*, lures in male bees with a perfumed oil; Majorca's beautiful bee orchid blossoms look and smell just like honey and are specially created to glue their pollen sacs onto bees' legs—thereby tricking the bees into unwittingly carrying the pollen from one flower to another.

Because their blooms are long lasting—often one to four weeks, depending upon the variety—orchids are a wise investment for a well-appointed corner of one's living space. In 1905, H. G. Wells commented on the flowering of the cymbidum: "Here slowly unfolds before the delighted eyes of the happy purchaser, day after day, some novel richness, a strange twist of the labellum, or some subtler coloration or unexpected mimicry. Pride, beauty, and profit blossom together on one delicate green spike, and it may be, even immortality."

This arrangement is almost foolproof, and perfect for the beginner. Several orchid varieties can be interchanged in this design, including the popular moth orchid, *phalaenopsis*, or one of the hundreds of species of genus *Oncidium* orchids. The key to this arrangement is the strategically placed orchid stems, overlapping both in the vase and outside of it. A hint of spiraled willow subtly complements the crossing of the orchid stems. First place the willow, followed by the orchids, noting carefully the look of each in relationship to the others. Allow for plenty of breathing space.

THE UNIVERSE
IN A SINGLE FLOWER

During Japan's Momoyama period (1573–1615), the refined, *nageire* style of flower arrangement came to symbolize the aesthetics of simple restraint, so condensed that a single flower could represent the life of all nature, and indeed the universe. This aesthetic of quiet, simple beauty, known as *wabi*, was often expressed in one single cherry blossom branch, standing upright in a vase.

This concept is often related in a simple story of two of Japan's most famous rulers of the period. Hideyoshi, upon hearing that the morning glories in Rikyu's private garden were in magnificent bloom, decided that he must see them, and made an appointment one day to call on Rikyu. When he arrived, the morning glories had all been cut down; not a single one remained. Disgruntled, Hideyoshi entered the teahouse, where he noticed a single morning glory arranged in a small vase—a bloom of such perfection that it both satisfied and overwhelmed him.

A single bloom speaks of refinement and cleanliness. Presenting only one place for the eye to rest, a single bloom

These rare, burnt orange "treasure" calla lilies are imported from New Zealand, giving this arrangement an upscale and unique look simply by virtue of their inclusion. In the draping of these lilies askew over one side of the container, there is a relaxing quality to the design. Keep the stems short when composing these, so that the flower heads peek over the side of the vessel. Try contrasting the elegance and purity of the lily with a hand-crafted, highly glazed pot.

Two long-stemmed pink peonies picked up at the farmers' market are a welcome addition to an impromptu Sunday brunch. Place each stem one at a time, paying attention to both the space between the flower heads and the space between the stems. Consider the completely different effect of a two-flower arrangement, as elegant ranunculus buds stretch forth their heads from a handthrown traditional Japanese vase. The vase was crafted by Bezen Yaki potters, an operation that has been firing pottery for more than 1,000 years.

is appreciated for everything it has to offer the onlooker: Color, shape, and texture abound in the flirtation of one single flower. Whether one selects one bright gerbera daisy or a single white lily, one really can't go wrong. Most single blooms are so aesthetically pleasing that they require nothing more of the arranger than to be fresh and well positioned.

In Japan, a room in the very humblest of houses will have in its place of honor—an alcove called the *tokonoma*—a flower vase. The Japanese flower vase is often made of the roughest and coarsest pottery, with irregular glaze and contour. Its very roughness or imperfection shows off by contrast the delicate flowers it contains. When you choose your bud vase, don't be afraid to explore this juxtaposition of vase and bloom. Whether you choose a long-forgotten jam jar or Baccarat crystal, have fun with your selections.

Here we experiment with a mint green antique porcelain bud vase, taking turns accenting it with a periwinkle hyacinth, a purple iris, a bi-colored rose, a few stems of the succulent aeonium, and two shocking pink gerbera daisies. Notice how each flower provides a completely different visual effect.

When selecting flowers, consider the subtleties that can be created by showcasing the flower's individual parts. The hyacinth will fragrantly fill any space in which one places it, holding its own ground, so to speak, by its beautiful scent and delicate flower. The leaves of this flower separate naturally, though a carefully prodding of the finger can nudge the most reluctant leaves to cooperate.

The angle of space created between the iris stem and its leaf is nature at its best. Though some ambitious designers might choose to clip these leaves in order to showcase only the stem and flower, retaining the leaves adds a dimension of space unachievable by any other measure. Though strong and definitive, the iris is not standing upright, but rather leans gently to one side, conveying both ease and motion. The flower arrangement is equally effective with both a closed iris bud and one that has opened.

One short red-and-cream bi-colored rose sits on top of the vase at full attention. Because only the flower is in view, the vase and bloom organically become one. The lack of space imposed by merging flower and vessel creates a unique synthesis; with no starting or ending point, the arrangement exudes infinity. This selection is perfect as a tub or wash-basin accent.

Though one might not think to juxtapose a fine ceramic vase with the roughness of a Southwestern succulent, it is its out-of-the-ordinary quality that makes this combination effective. One single aeonium rosette, with its elegant curved stem, showcases the beauty of the plant.

It's no wonder that gerbera daisies have often been called the happiest flower in the world. With their heads pointed upward, they wait to greet the most discerning onlooker with a smile. The wave of the stems creates a fluidity to this arrangement that would be lacking otherwise; selecting two flowers instead of one creates a beautiful space between the two. The natural inclination to wire these gerberas would not only cut off the circulatory flow of water to the bud, it would also interfere with the natural arc of the stem and create an undesirable stiffness to the arrangement.

SINGULAR FLOWERS EN MASSE

Filling a vessel with a mass of one type of flower creates a visual impact that can reach beyond that of an individual bloom. This variation on the single-flower concept is relatively straightforward: It involves arranging multiple stems of the same flower in either a single vessel or several of them. This striking look of unified or slightly varied color complements a number of flowers, including lisianthus, tulips, hyacinth, narcissus, iceland poppies, peonies, ranunculus, and sweet peas, and looks least forced when in-season flowers are chosen.

Same-flower designs take little skill to assemble. The key lies in selecting fresh flowers. These types of arrangements are most visually pleasing if the buds are in various stages of opening, so that the presentation changes appearance slightly over time and continues to have life for several days as the tighter buds begin to open.

The white lilac is one of the most effective flowers to group en masse, because its delicate flowers and intricate stems create an interesting use of space, especially when viewed within a glass vessel. The positioning of six delicate starfish provides a grid for inserting the stems and conveys the illusion that the lilac is growing in harmony with the sea life. Juxtaposing the flowers and the starfish gives the arrangement depth, beckoning the onlooker to reach out and touch it.

French long-stemmed white tulips are most striking when cast almost offhandedly into an antique mint green vase. The *nouveau élégance* created by harmonizing the flowers and vessel factors heavily into this design's overall effect. The natural shape of the tulip's stem allows for a very fluid arrangement, its gently opening leaves creating a more substantial "base" for the delicacy of the bud. Because tulips are available at a moment's notice at virtually every flower stall or grocer's stand, they are the perfect accompaniment to a last-minute dinner party.

An interesting aside: Originally, there were a total of nine tulips in this design, but we decided—after taking a few steps back from the arrangement—that it was more effective with only seven. So we pulled two out. Key to any intuitive designer is knowing when to stop.

AMAZING CALLA LILIES

Landmarked by the Art Nouveau movement, arum or calla lilies are enjoying a resurgence in popularity as people yearn for simplification. These timeless and elegant stems have a classic quality about them, making them perfect for a simple arrangement of three or a more elaborate design of twenty. Deep black calla lilies are the flower *du jour* for this "progression" arrangement, which demonstrates that the life force of the flower increases as the sparse is built upon. Rather than simply "adding" flowers to the vase, the Zen arranger is sensitive to the construction of a piece of work, the result of which is intentional yet unpretentious.

From a spiritual viewpoint, the concept of void within nature represents the Buddhist concept of *ku*. Open space allows for great creativity, both within a working environment and within the arrangement itself. To embrace this concept, try standing back from your arrangement and taking pause. The Japanese poet Basho said, "When we observe things calmly, we notice that all things have their fulfillment." Allow yourself to create unhurriedly. Don't be afraid to move around your arrangement, view it from different angles, and adjust the flowers according to a different perspective.

The following photographs are a guide to putting together both simplified and complex designs. But don't be tied to these images. Without calling upon your own inner artist, your result is destined to be stiff and lifeless, for you will be parroting a photograph rather than drawing upon its instructive wisdom to guide you. In this regard, it is perhaps best to contemplate the words of Ching Hao: "He who tries to transmit the spirit by obtaining the outward appearance will produce a dead thing."

Three fresh calla lilies are used in a design that can effectively stand alone or become the basis for a much grander effort. Note the use of space created between the stems' natural wave, courtesy of Mother Nature.

The flexible willow twisted into the base of this arrangement not only creates an interesting spatial relationship, but also supplies a sturdy base for the three stems to secure themselves in. Simply lay hold of a few branches of fresh willow and bend them into a tighter bunch; place inside a glass vase of your choosing.

Building upon the initial design of three, here a total of five lilies fan out. Notice that these particular lilies have two flower heads per stem, adding a unique quality to their appearance. While you may be tempted to choose a more "perfect" flower, try incorporating these oddities of nature; your arrangement will look all the more natural for it. Indeed, take comfort in this fact: In each of the nearly one million floral species that grace planet Earth, no two blossoms are identical.

A few more stems are added. Notice the natural arcing of the stem. Because flowers are living beings, they respond to touch. The heat of your hand and a gentle massage will shape the stem into a greater arc.

Still more stems are added. Even as you fill the vase, be conscious not to let the space get lost.

A few more stems accentuate the natural flow of the stems and fanlike shape of the arrangement.

The grand finale! Approximately 50 lilies are used in this elaborate creation. Notice how the space first created among the three blooms in our original arrangement has not been compromised. As important, proportion can be seen in every aspect of this final design: proportion of the flowers in relation to one another, and proportion of the complete design in relation to the vase. The result is a balanced effect that is free-flowing, fresh, and *alive*.

MORE IS ZEN

The "mixed bouquet," to borrow a Western expression, was derived from the grower's desire to mix different types of flowers together in one bundle for a point-of-purchase sale. While multiple flowers of various sizes, shapes, textures, and hues can produce Zen arrangements, care must be taken in selecting *complementary* flowers, and never too many in type or number.

Replicating shape or evoking a monochromatic color scheme can produce a mesmerizing effect that is very restful to the eye. Peonies, hydrangea, roses, marigolds, sweet William, and chrysanthemums are all good examples of flowers that can produce a dominant, enclosed shape.

Because color has a definite effect on human senses, bright, striking results can be achieved by using warm colors, such as reds, oranges, and warmer yellows (known as "hot," or advancing colors, and the ones we chose for this arrangement), while more soothing designs can be created by selecting "cool," or receding, colors, such as pinks, mauves, blues, and purples. In either case, the result is a Zen twist on the traditional English garden bouquet.

The ceremonial shaman feathers placed on the Deco entryway furnishing provide the inspiration for the color and composition of this mixed bouquet. Tiny lime green protea, with fernlike, delicate leaves reminiscent of the feathers of a bird, meet bells-of-Ireland and sexy, pink haliconia. Bright orange aloe blossoms, indigenous to South Africa and abundant in the Southwestern United States, up the ante on this vibrant composition. Completing the look are two stems of Costa Rican "parakeet" haliconia. Notice how the vase echoes the color and pattern of the bureau's wood; the flowers are an extension of both the vase and the oil painting against which they are positioned.

THE LOTUS BLOSSOM

All of Asia has some 60,000 species of plants, approximately one sixth of the world's known flora. Many of the United States' most familiar ornamental plants originated in China and Japan, including azalea, rhododendron, camellia, gardenia, hibiscus, peony, chrysanthemum, and ginkgo. Steeped in centuries of tradition and appreciation, Asians have attributed aesthetic, spiritual, and mystical significance to many of their species.

This is perhaps most true for the lotus. For the Asian culture, this plant is the symbol of purity, immortality, and tranquility. Gazing toward heaven, the lotus lifts itself up from turbid water and a muddy earth, and presents itself as a perfect specimen, in clear white or pink color, surrounded by perfectly shining bright green leaves. For the Buddhist, the lotus represents a noble character, the soul battling against the material world to reach the light. It is also a Confucian model for the enlightened person. At night the flower closes and sinks underwater, at dawn it rises and opens again. According to one creation myth, it was a giant lotus that first rose out of the watery chaos at the beginning of time.

The lotus is the only botanical that pollinates and seeds itself simultaneously. While other flowers need a bee, a bird, or the wind to carry its seed, the lotus does it internally. As such, the lotus blossom symbolizes the inseparability of cause and effect. The lotus is also valued for its dramatic blue-green foliage, which spans the seasons from late summer into autumn, when the leaves change to withered browns with the first frost.

Equally noted are lotus pods. Nichiren Daishonin, 12th century Japanese priest, wrote, "The pure lotus flower blooms out of the muddy pond, the fragrant sandalwood grows from the soil." The fragrance of its blossom spread far and wide though it always stood still and strong. Once the flowers died, the pods could be used for decorative purposes, the seeds for medicinal ones. A Song dynasty herbal medicine book notes the seeds' exceptional vitality, saying that lotus seeds eaten and then excreted by wild geese could sprout even after several years, and those brought into mountain caves by birds could remain alive as long as some three hundred years.

Three lotus blossoms stand tall and erect in a square stone vessel. To aid the stems in standing tall, some well-soaked floral foam has been cut and placed in the container prior to assembling. This design is minimalist in its color, structure, and containment, the result having a very soothing effect on the senses. The three lotus mirror the Zen Principle of Three, which states that the universe can be divided into three realms—heaven, earth, and the world of men.

The addition of a single open lotus blossom, cut low, anchors the arrangement and adds a pop of color.

CARE & CONDITIONING

Flowers seem intended for the solace of ordinary humanity. —John Ruskin

Fresh water and proper placement are essential to a long-lasting Zen flower design. Most flower arrangements, such as those that incorporate roses, peonies, and lilies, have a shelf life of about four to five days; others, which include orchids and anthuriums, can remain fresh up to two full weeks. Essential to a design's beauty and life is the care one gives it—knowing how to maintain and enjoy the arrangement while sensitively recognizing its needs.

At The Flower Box, it has been our experience that—next to clean, fresh water—the most important factor in the beauty and longevity of flowers is the manner in which they are touched. Nothing goes further than a loving touch and an appreciation for the grace and magic that flowers impart to everyone who encounters them. People repeatedly ask us why our flowers last so much longer than those they have purchased elsewhere. We are certain that the reason is our undying love for the flowers we purvey.

CHANGING THE WATER

The most important factor in the life of any cut flower is the availability of fresh, clean water. A flower is made primarily of water and it must be able to drink freely at all times to have an optimal life span. Days-old water provides a breeding ground for microscopic bacteria. These bacteria attach themselves to the stem ends and block the flow of water up to the flower heads. One should always change the vase water regularly—even daily—to decrease the rate at which bacteria breed.

With very large and/or intricate designs, do not try to empty the water or tip over the arrangement in a way that might disturb the design. Instead, take the arrangement outside and use a garden hose to refill it. Place the hose in the vessel and gently flush out the old water and fill it with new, making sure to dry the sides and bottom of the vessel before restoring it to its place. With smaller arrangements, the same procedure works well with the kitchen-sink faucet; the key here is not to disturb the design while completing your objective of refueling the arrangement.

For glass vases, it is best to change the water as soon as it becomes cloudy. This helps to control the odors and reduce the growth of bacteria. Adding a very small amount of bleach to the water will reduce the growth of bacteria as well, and is especially helpful in an arrangement where changing the water is impossible or difficult. Some flowers, such as alliums or stock, have a naturally offensive odor and can begin to smell strongly when the water is older. Adding bleach to these flowers is always beneficial; most vases need just a few drops or up to $1/2$ teaspoon for more pungent varieties.

with flowers such as poinsettias, be especially careful to dry off the leaves. Similarly, petals that are particularly fragile will spot if too much water is left on them. You can remove the excess moisture by shaking it off or patting it dry.

RECUTTING STEMS

Stems are essential for water and food transportation, and provide support for the leaves and flowers. One might say that the life force of a flower is in its stem; the stem of a flower can reveal much about the variety itself, as well as what the flower needs. Changing the container's water and recutting your flowers' stems are the most important things one must do for flowers to thrive and express their full beauty.

For most flowers, particularly those that are starting to droop or wilt prematurely, simply recut the bottom of the stem about $1/4$ inch and reset. If it is not possible to remove the flower, place a plastic bag over the head of the flower to create a humidity chamber, which almost magically revives the bloom.

Always use a floral knife or shears when working with your arrangement. Do not cut your flowers with a typical pair of household scissors, as they will actually crush the stems, closing the veins to water uptake rather than facilitating it. It is essential to cut the stem at an angle, as this facilitates more water absorption. A stem cut straight across rests on the bottom of the vessel; this reduces the flower's ability to drink properly.

MISTING

Many flowers love a light misting after the arrangement is complete. Some flowers, such as hydrangea, drink from their heads, or petals, and must be sprayed frequently in order to maintain their perkiness. When misting, let the water drip off and settle before returning your design to its destination. Take care not to place anything wet on special surfaces—always check the bottom of the vessel before returning it to its home. It is a good idea to place the finished arrangement on a cork mat, which one can purchase at a garden center or home improvement store and which are available in all shapes and sizes.

If the leaves of a plant are fuzzy, they may spot if you allow water to drop on them. When refreshing an arrangement

HARD STEMS: To expose the soft inner tissue of the stem and ensure water absorption, it is a good idea to crush gently the outer hard stem with a hammer or slit it with a sharp knife. While you have done this in preparing your arrangement, you may need to recut and recrush your stems, especially when working with flowers like lilac and dogwood.

SOFT STEMS: Soft stems, such as bulbs, absorb water easily. Take care not to overwater them, and be sure to arrange them in shallow water so they do not become sodden.

WOODEN STEMS: For blossoms with wooden stems, scrape off about 2 inches of bark on the bottom of the stem before crushing or splitting, as this allows maximum water intake.

HOLLOW STEMS: For flowers with hollow stems, such as amaryllis, try holding the stem upside down, filling it with water, and then plugging it with cotton before placing in the design. This method holds the water for a longer period of time, and you'll need to change the vase water less frequently.

MILKY STEMS: Some flowers, such as poppies, poinsettias, campanula, hollyhock hydrangeas, and euphorbias, let out a milky substance when cut, forming a seal and preventing the flow of water. When designing with this type of flower, immerse the stem in boiling water for 10 seconds or so, to prevent the sealing, then arrange as usual. Another method for sealing the stem involves cauterizing the cut by holding a match or lighter to the stem. The milky substance is latex, so be sure to wash your hands after handling these stems, and keep them away from your eyes.

Always have your container of water ready and waiting and place your flowers back in the water as soon as you have cut them. Sometimes we cut the flowers under water; this does seem helpful, if a bit laborious. The key is to get the stem back into water quickly—only a few minutes out of water and the flower will scab over the cut, which will prevent it from taking up water.

REMOVING EXCESS FOLIAGE

In any arrangement, some flower heads naturally will die before others. Always remove these heads quickly, so as to send the life force back into the stem to feed the emerging blossoms. Similarly, be sure to snip off any excess leaves or withered foliage—for both aesthetic and health reasons. Additionally, always remove extraneous leaves *below* the water level, as the submerged leaves will contribute to bacteria growth. Remember, the water needs to travel up the stem to the flower head, and too much foliage along the way can prevent the blossom from receiving all it needs.

WORKING WITH YOUR MATERIALS

In general, arrangements in florist foam maintain water longer; however, it is a good idea to "top off" these arrangements by adding fresh water after two to three days, making sure not to overflow your vessel. (Note that some flowers with delicate stems do not do well in florist foam.) Flowers in tubes need checking every two days to make sure the water is still surrounding the stem. Tubes can easily be emptied and refilled. Flowers in pin holders need to have the water covering the pin at all times, which can be achieved simply by adding fresh water to your arrangement.

CONDITIONS TO AVOID

Any condition that causes water to be lost from the flower, such as a heating system, dry air, or light and heat from the sun, or anything that prevents the flower from taking up or drinking water, will shorten the life of the flower.

HEAT: When flowers are exposed to heat, they age at a greater rate than at lower temperatures. The cooler the room or location in which they are displayed, the longer they will last. While we love arrangements to enhance the corner of a kitchen counter or the breakfast table, bear in mind that the kitchen tends to be a warm—even hot—area. When arranging a design for this room, it is a good idea to select flowers that enjoy the sunshine and warmth when in their natural environment, such as calla lilies, agapanthus, freesias, and ranunculus.

SUNLIGHT: Arrangements exposed to direct sunlight can easily become overheated, succumbing to the increased rate of development and the drying out of their petals. A cool, dark environment is best for your Zen arrangement.

COLD CONDITIONS: Internal flower cells can become damaged if subjected to very low temperatures. Orchids, anthuriums, and other tropical flowers that originated in a humid, warm climate are particularly susceptible to low-temperature damage. If the temperature drops anywhere below 40 degrees, flowers must be wrapped or somehow insulated to keep them from freezing. When encountering a drafty locale—such as a hallway or open door—petals tend to dry out prematurely. Avoid these locations if you want your arrangement to thrive.

AIR CONDITIONING: Zen arrangements placed in large office buildings with aggressive air conditioning systems tend to dry out very quickly. This is particularly true for flowers that have large, exposed petals, such as daisies, roses, peonies, and hydrangeas.

Acknowledgments

The authors would like to thank the following people for their support during the production of this book: Deborah Yost, our acquiring editor at Stewart, Tabori & Chang; Senior Editor Jennifer Levesque; and Senior Designer Julie Hoffer. Thanks to our agent Ellen Geiger; photographer Emily Brooke Sandor; wordsmith Gina Misiroglu; and entire staff of The Flower Box of Santa Monica, California.

In addition, we are grateful for the following people and business establishments whose lives have touched us in many ways: Lynda Vance and Norman Cohen; Kate Capshaw Spielberg and Steven Spielberg; Kathleen Kennedy and Frank Marshall; Lani and Herb Alpert; Sherri and Michael Crichton; Leah Adler; Miriam and Tom Schulman; Cydney and Gary Mandel; Lynne and Mark Leventen; Nancy Fish; Judy Sadowski; Akwa Restaurant; Marion Brayton; Stephanie Sydney; Daisaku and Mrs Ikeda and the S.G.I. global family; Ashley Rogers; Diane Black; Steven Levine and California Institute of the Arts; Katie Gallagher and Sandy Brokaw; Barbara and the late Marvin Davis; the late Dodi Al Fayed; Nobu Matsuhisa; Winston Brock Chappell; Bronya Galef; Lee Ann and John Sauter; Judith Kanner and Kanner Architects; Deborah and Gabriel Brener; Rita Pynoos; Kat and Gregory Montegna; Matilda Buck; Bonnie Hamilton; Faye Greene; Yoko Maeda; Francisco Gomez; Liane Douglas; Clemente Gomez; Nextali Moreira; Nazgol Lolachi; Rhona Ross; Alana Sweetwater; Rebecca Fearing; Marjorie Mcilwain; Gregg and Fredo Sutton; Matt Quave; Bradon Winslow; Debbie Schauer; Domini Carrington; Cindy Laudati; Martha Naim; The Lazzarino family; Marina Santis; The Burr Family; Cheryl Pistone; Deanne Roseanne; Jerry Packard; David Shamsa; Patty Clary, Alternatives to toxics.

For her beautiful handcrafted vessels, thanks to Tali Ilan.

Finally, heartfelt thanks for their love and support and inspiration:

John Velmore Herron; Katyrose Berkley Herron; Helen and Fred Berkley; David and Diania Berkley; Ruth and Jim Arnold; Beverly Berkley and Tim Dant; JC; Hiroshi Kitamura; The Dziubinski Family; The Kitamura Family.

SELECTED RESOURCES

BOOKS: *Some fabulous reading, information on plants, tips on arranging flowers, and ideas for creating your own special sanctuaries can be found in these books.*

Arnold, Peter. *Orchids.* New York: Rizzoli, 1994.

Church, Thomas Dolliver. *Gardens Are for People: How to Plan for Outdoor Living*, 3rd ed. Berkeley: University of California Press, 1995.

Cox, Jeff. *Landscaping with Nature.* Emmaus, PA: Rodale, 1991.

Fairchild, David. *The World Was My Garden: Travels of a Plant Explorer.* New York: Charles Scribner's Sons, 1945.

Hart, Sunniva. *Zen Gardening.* New York: Stewart, Tabori, & Chang, 1999.

Imes, Rick. *Wildflowers: How to Identify Flowers in the Wild and How to Grow Them in Your Garden.* Emmaus, PA: Rodale, 1992.

Lee, Vinny. Zen Interiors. New York: Stewart, Tabori, & Chang, 1999.

L. H. Bailey Hortorium. *Hortus Third: A Concise Dictionary of Plants Cultivated in the United States and Canada.* New York: Macmillan, 1976.

Smaus, *Robert. Plants and Planting the Garden.* New York: Abrams, 1989.

Sunset Western Garden Book. Menlo Park, CA: Sunset Publishing, 2001.

Verey, Rosemary. The Flower Arranger's Garden. Boston: Little, Brown, 1989.

Waters, George, and Nora Harlow. *The Pacific Horticulture Book of Western Gardening.* Boston: David R. Godine, 1990.

Wilson, Jim. *Landscaping with Herbs.* Boston: Houghton Mifflin Co, 1994.

WEBSITES: *Great on-line resources exist to aid you in floral selection, design, products, and healing.*

American Horticulture Society:
www.ahs.org

American Institute of Floral Designers:
www.aifd.org

Dr. Edward Bach and the Bach Flower Remedies: www.bachcentre.com

Garden Plant Care:
www.gardenplantcare.com

Society of American Florists:
www.aboutflowers.com

Wholesale Florist and Florist Supplier Association: www.wffsa.org

The Flower Box, located just a stone's throw from the Pacific Ocean in Santa Monica, California, welcomes the passer-by to enter and soak up some of the amazing healing properties of the varied, fragrant, and strikingly beautiful botanicals housed within. A dose of the best Mother Nature has to provide is what proprietor Brenda Berkley and staff aim to provide— inspiring all who enter to lift and enliven their hearts and homes. Every design is uniquely created for each customer with his or her specific needs in mind.
www.theflowerbox.com

INDEX